# Transmediality in Independent Journalism

*Transmediality in Independent Journalism* investigates mainstream journalism and its escape routes to independence through transmedia strategies. Within the scope of the latest debates in Turkey, the author argues that the function of transmediality in Turkish journalism is gradually shifting from being only a commercial entity to becoming a political system for social change, a survival mechanism for independent journalists to reach out to diverse audiences, and gain back the public trust.

Bringing a fresh perspective to recent studies on cultures of transmediality along with an in-depth analysis of three contemporary Turkish cases, the book:

- Builds upon questions of whether transmedia storytelling can offer a support system to construct an alternative news media world in a political context such as Turkey's
- Examines how transmedia storytelling can reach places the mainstream news media can't control
- Explores whether transmedia storytelling can sustain the survival of an independent journalist in Turkey's political context

Looking beyond the case of Turkey, this study will be an important addition to the literature on rethinking journalistic form and practice, teaching transmedia strategies, and social communication. It will be of great benefit to students and scholars of journalism studies, transmedia studies, and media and communication studies.

**Dilek Gürsoy** is a research assistant in the Media and Communication Department at Istanbul Bilgi University, Turkey.

# Routledge Advances in Transmedia Studies

*Series Editor: Matthew Freeman*

This series publishes monographs and edited collections that sit at the cutting-edge of today's interdisciplinary cross-platform media landscape. Topics should consider emerging transmedia applications in and across industries, cultures, arts, practices, or research methodologies. The series is especially interested in research exploring the future possibilities of an interconnected media landscape that looks beyond the field of media studies, notably broadening to include socio-political contexts, education, experience design, mixed-reality, journalism, the proliferation of screens, as well as art- and writing-based dimensions to do with the role of digital platforms like VR, apps and iDocs to tell new stories and express new ideas across multiple platforms in ways that join up with the social world.

**Transmediality in Independent Journalism**
The Turkish Case
*Dilek Gürsoy*

# Transmediality in Independent Journalism
## The Turkish Case

**Dilek Gürsoy**

Routledge
Taylor & Francis Group

LONDON AND NEW YORK

First published 2020
by Routledge
2 Park Square, Milton Park, Abingdon, Oxon OX14 4RN

and by Routledge
605 Third Avenue, New York, NY 10017

First issued in paperback 2022

*Routledge is an imprint of the Taylor & Francis Group, an informa business*

*British Library Cataloguing-in-Publication Data*
A catalogue record for this book is available from the British Library

*Library of Congress Cataloging-in-Publication Data*
A catalog record has been requested for this book

ISBN 13: 978-1-03-240038-9 (pbk)
ISBN 13: 978-0-367-85913-8 (hbk)
ISBN 13: 978-1-003-01574-1 (ebk)

DOI: 10.4324/9781003015741

Typeset in Times New Roman
by codeMantra

To my mom and dad, who are eager to become grandparents. Here is your first grandchild.

# Contents

# Acknowledgements

It is, perhaps, every young scholar's dream to have a book of his/her own, featured by an esteemed publisher. At least it was a dream that I had and believed to be far from reality. Dr. Matthew Freeman realised this dream by believing in me. For that, I would like to express to him my utmost gratitude because I know for sure that this book would not have existed without his trust in me.

Giving life to a book is a very challenging process. One must overcome so many obstacles that sometimes it is hard to imagine doing it alone. That is why I am eternally grateful to Professor Aslı Tunç for holding the bright light of guidance in the utter darkness of this course. Her feedback and contributions have taught me so much and continues to do so.

In this difficult journey, one also craves for emotional support. A support that is not visible to the eye but nourishes the author with productive motivation. Therefore, I offer my appreciation to Associate Professor Nazan Haydari, Müge İplikçi Çakır, and my dear friend and office mate Birol Şevki Tavlı for being there whenever I needed their help. I know that my enjoyment in writing this book would perish without their blessings.

As understood so far, this research is not the product of a single person, especially when its content relies on experiences of others. For this research, Ruşen Çakır, Ünsal Ünlü, and Nadire Mater did not hesitate to give their valuable time from their busy schedules. I would like to thank them for their contributions that gave life to and enriched the content of this research.

I cannot thank Chole Current enough for her genuine support in hiding the fact that English is not my mother tongue.

I am also grateful to Suzanne Richardson as the editor and Sukriti Pandey as the editor assistant of Routledge. Their assistance has considerably eased this challenging process.

Last but not least, I would like to thank my parents, Hadiye and Deniz Gürsoy, also my brother Derin for supporting me every step of the way.

# 1 Introduction

"Hope" is the thing with feathers -
That perches in the soul -
And sings the tune without the words -
And never stops - at all -

And sweetest - in the Gale - is heard -
And sore must be the storm -
That could abash the little Bird
That kept so many warm -

I've heard it in the chillest land -
And on the strangest Sea -
Yet - never - in Extremity,
It asked a crumb - of me.

—Emily Dickinson, "Hope"

There are so many ways to describe what the term *transmediality* stands for. In the world of storytelling, it is the new kid on the block, attractive but requires knowing from every aspect. When I say "new", I only refer to its recent popularity in the academic realm. As a matter of fact, transmediality is a practice that is considered to have a long history (Freeman, 2016). However, it was only popularly defined in the early 2000s, by Henry Jenkins (2006), as a method of constructing a participative storyworld, where each medium reveals unique information to the audience. Presently, after many years of enquiry and evolution, transmediality is much more. It is the immersive language of industries, arts, practices, cultures, and methodologies (Freeman & Gambarato, 2018). On a more abstract level, it is a way of communicating, understanding, and, in some cultures, solving complex issues (Freeman & Proctor, 2018). These definitions reflect only some of what researchers have come up with. The rest is up to further investigation, such as this one, to dig deeper into the unknowns of transmedia studies.

Therefore, one of the scholarly incentives behind this investigation is to contribute to the ongoing debate about future directions of transmediality. To narrow the scope, the following study approaches this field within the confines of journalism. The reason behind this choice is twofold. Firstly, journalism in the 21st century has become a widely discussed topic all around the world. Global debates about fake news, post-truth, and digital transformation position journalism studies in the pile of attractive fields to investigate. Secondly, transmediality in journalism is still a perspective that needs to be developed. News media, journalism practice, journalists, and news consumers are transforming each day with the advances in media technologies. Moreover, each country has its own journalism culture (Phillips, 2014). This line of thought opens the door to new meanings offered by the technological change and cultural differences.

This brings us to the next purpose of this research: analysing independent journalism initiatives in Turkey through the lens of transmediality. What this book sets out to discover is the role of transmediality in a specific context. It aims to relocate what we already know about this concept and apply it to the problematic journalism environment within Turkey. The chosen context of this book calls to question whether transmediality can bring hope to the deteriorating faith of journalism practice. Where distrust and fear distort truths and ethics in the mainstream journalism practices, can transmediality be a support system to reconstruct an alternative news environment? While the government rules the mainstream with an iron fist, can transmedia strategies help to conquer unregulated news spaces? Last but not least, struggling to defend the public's right to information, can transmediality help sustain the survival of independent journalists?

The following chapter, Chapter 2, constructs the contextual environment of this study. It starts with painting a global picture of the shifts in the contemporary journalism practice. Along the way, it identifies certain traits of this transforming news culture. The chapter then moves towards a specific geography, Turkey, where it exposes the current state of the country's mainstream media and explains the reasons behind the formations of independent journalism initiatives. Chapter 3, followingly, sets off to build conceptual bridges between notions of independent journalism and transmedia journalism. In this pursuit, it presents how transmedia narratives manifest in journalism practices, how the notion of transmedia ethos plays a part in culturally uniting an interactive society, and how the initiatives of independent journalism in Turkey relate to the overall structural and cultural aspects of transmediality. This chapter dwells upon these areas to highlight the vital role of transmediality in journalism, especially from the fresh perspective of Turkey. Chapter 4 utilises the principles, concepts, and relations, discussed in Chapter 3, to demonstrate the position of transmediality in three different independent journalism initiatives in Turkey. Based on face-to-face interviews with the founders of these initiatives, the chapter analyses these distinct cases to understand their histories, objectives, operational structures, and connection to their communities. Moreover, it lays bare the pillars of sustainability for each case to show how these initiatives survive. The chapter goes through with a detailed demonstration of why transmediality plays a vital role for the chosen cases. The last chapter, Chapter 5, brings the study to an end by looking beyond the case of Turkey to draw conclusions for transmedia journalists more broadly and invites young scholars of Turkey to join the global conversation of transmediality.

## References

Freeman, M. (2016). *Historicising Transmedia Storytelling: Early Twentieth-Century Transmedia Story Worlds*. Routledge.

Freeman, M., & Gambarato, R. R. (Eds.). (2018). *The Routledge Companion to Transmedia Studies*. Routledge.

Freeman, M., & Proctor, W. (Eds.). (2018). *Global Convergence Cultures: Transmedia Earth*. Routledge.

Jenkins, H. (2006). *Convergence Culture: Where Old and New Media Collide*. NYU Press.

Phillips, A. (2014). *Journalism in Context: Practice and Theory for the Digital Age*. Routledge.

# 2   Dethreading of a practice

**Dethreading**
(n.) any process in which the threaded structure of a molecule is disrupted.

(YourDictionary, n.d.)

The disruption has been in the making long before the sirens. It shouldn't have been hard to foresee what was about to happen to a practice that has always depended on the media technologies of its time. Nevertheless, it arrived with a bang that no one anticipated. Journalism became a practice to be reconsidered.

In an era of technological, social, and cultural conversion, a flood of constant change has worn away the roots of journalism practice. These worn out roots extend along questions relating to ethics, function, and position of journalists. In the academic field, scholars of media studies keep a watchful eye on press freedom under titles relating to media and democracy, while scholars of internet studies and political science scrutinise questions about internet freedom, fake news, post-truth, and censorship. In this changing order, contemporary journalism initiatives welcome new methods to convey the news to audiences, such as citizen participation, multiple and cross-media storytelling, and self-governance.

Meanwhile in Turkey, along with global concerns on the future of their practice, journalists face a political barrier, where the political establishment maintains full control of the mainstream news media. One by one, critical news about the government are silenced, leaving mainstream media shorn of truth, investigation, and press freedom. The political oppression forces blacklisted journalists to look for other occupations or, in some dedicated cases, practice journalism in alternative news media outlets.

Now, we are at a threshold that is shaking the core of journalism practice. That is why this chapter's title refers to the process of *dethreading*, a term of organic chemistry. The molecule of journalism is disrupted, and the definition of journalism and its surrounding ecology is in constant change. A famous quote from the Greek philosopher Heraclitus says, "No man ever steps in the same river twice, for it's not the same river and he's not the same man". Leaving its shed skin behind, journalism is in transition again to face the new challenges of convergent news media production and technologies, participative audiences, and increasing authoritative barriers of oppressive governments.

This chapter sets out to explore some of the global fractures that disrupted the molecule of journalism practice. Examining these fractures is crucial in forming epistemological questions on the role of transmediality in reconsidering a new journalistic perspective. The chapter then moves into a more specific geography. Turkey's mainstream media environment is put under a lens to determine the context of this research. Within this context, unique values and beliefs surrounding and within Turkish independent journalism initiatives become significant. Their significance lies in conceptualising what is now referred to as the *transmedia ethos*,[1] which will be dwelled upon in Chapter 3.

## An interfluent affair

Change comes in many forms and sizes, and it shines with a global and significant impact on the practice of journalism from multiple angles. Producing, reporting, and consuming news turned into a new experience in the age of convergent media technologies for the globally social audiences (Gambarato & Tarcia, 2017; Heinrich, 2011). The ambiguous door of the 21st century opened to new questions relating to the identity, authority, purpose, and practice of journalists. Scholars of journalism, media, political science, and internet studies have previously scrutinised, and, still to this day, continue to explore what is in motion, and where journalism is heading to (see Carson, 2019; Hanitzsch, Hanusch, Ramaprasad, & de Beer, 2019; Price, 2019; Wahl-Jorgensen & Hanitzsch, 2019).

The aim of this section is to outline the recent state around and within journalism practice. In other words, paint a picture of the interfluent chaos that is prevalent in the journalism scene. What I mean by *interfluence* is the act of entities flowing together and intervening with each other to form new entities. In the process, formerly drawn clear conceptual borders cease to exist, leaving chaos and uncertainty to form new definitions, behaviours, or systems.

## Interfluence of definitions

Current transformation in the global practice of journalism brings about new perspectives that yield new questions. One of these questions could relate to the interchanging definitions and actors within the news-making milieu. Perhaps, pursuit of this query may reveal how this chaotic but connected news environment plays along with notions of transmediality. To that end, this section addresses the dethreading of formerly distinct definitions and actors of journalism through interfluent dichotomies, such as fact *vs.* fiction, journalist *vs.* activist, and news maker *vs.* news consumer.

## Truth and trust

The interplay between fact and fiction has always been at the forefront in debates of journalism studies. A century-old investigation still echoes the same questions till this day: What is journalistic truth? How should a journalist attain and present it? A part of this longstanding effort can be seen as a journalist's attempt to maintain the trust of citizens. However, questions on truth and its representation have gained a more complex ground in today's journalism scene, correspondingly, constructing different conceptions of trust.

We are not strangers to the interplay between fact and fiction in journalism practices. Works of literary journalism have always let a pinch of fiction leak into factual events of a news story. However, in some cases, journalists may have gone too far in the limits of their imaginations. Evidently, there have been numerous instances where fabrication of news content made significant cracks in the foundation of trust in the news media. Time constraints and competitive pressures within the journalistic milieu have been the excuses of Janet Cooke,[2] Stephen Glass,[3] Michael Finkel,[4] Claas Relotius,[5] and many more as they confessed to their acts of news fabrication.

Although deliberate fabrication of news by professional journalists shakes the core of public trust, there is a more powerful earthquake that is disrupting the definition of truth and trust in the news media today. Truth, in the most absolute sense, is perhaps an impossible goal to reach. However, journalistic truth, as Kovach and Rosenstiel (2014) indicate, can be observed as rather a practical form of truth. Positioned in a social context, journalistic truth can be considered as a "sorting-out process" that initiates with a news story and then gains its functional truth as it is kneaded through society's "procedures and processes" (Kovach & Rosenstiel, 2014, p. 55):

> The truth is a complicated and sometimes contradictory phenomenon, but if it is seen as a process over time, journalism can get at it. First by stripping information of any attached misinformation, disinformation, or self-promoting bias and then by letting the community react, in the sorting-out process that ensues. As always, the search for truth becomes a conversation.
>
> (Kovach & Rosenstiel, 2014, p. 58)

However, this conversation is interrupted by the increasing pace in news gathering, pollution of false information, and persuasion tactics of commercial or political segments (Hirst, 2011). Convergent communication technologies enable news to be produced and consumed instantly, globally, and participatively. These circumstances not only diminish objective methods of verification,[6] but they also appear to facilitate fake-news pollution and alternative definitions of truth (Bossio, 2017; Fisher, 2018; Kovach & Rosenstiel, 2014; Phillips, 2014). The news industry, desperate to maintain revenue, allows commercial content to be disguised as news, or rather as fake news (Hirst, 2011). Moreover, taking advantage of the chaotic media environment of the digitally convergent era, political leaders utilise social media and pro-government news outlets to "influence the news agenda and public opinion of particular issues" (Bossio, 2017, p. 141). News about Angela Merkel's call for European Union (EU) army to defend Europe,[7] or the assault[8] of a headscarved woman and her baby in Turkey, exemplify only a fraction of an increasing decline of the journalism estate on a global scale. As an eye opening matter to this serious problem, Donald Trump's statements, before, during and after his 2016 election campaign for the US presidency, are commonly referenced cases in recent global research on fake news and the conception of truth in journalism (Gillers, 2018; Happer, Hoskins, & Merrin, 2018; Peters, Rider, Hyvönen, & Besley, 2018).

The affair between real and fake has come to a point where the perception of truth has been attacked by claims of "alternative facts" (Bossio, 2017, p. 142). As the 2016 word of the year, the term "post-truth" demonstrates how these alternative facts can construct a different conception of trust among a community of shared values and beliefs (Bossio, 2017; Fisher, 2018; Kovach & Rosenstiel, 2014). However, this is only one of many possible influences. A historical overview by Fisher (2018) on conceptions of news trust states that this conceptual shift may have occurred due to various reasons:

> Firstly, despite the volume of research on this topic there is no agreed definition or measure of 'trust' in news media. What is clear is that the common usage definition of 'reliability' and 'truth' no longer capture the multiple characteristics that can influence a consumer's perception of trust in news media. Secondly, there is a growing disconnection between the normative ideal of an informed citizenry and the complex range of motivations that can also have an impact on perceptions of news credibility in the digital era. Thirdly, there is a growing tension between the ideal of citizens being able to trust the information provided by the news media, and the urgent need for the public become more media literate and questioning of the information they access. In an age of uncertainty about the veracity of online information and the push for greater media literacy, is trust in news the desired goal? Or, should the 'art of sceptical knowing' (Kovach & Rosenstiel, 2010) be the new ideal?
>
> (Fisher, 2018, p. 33)

The binding line between truth and trust is no longer clearly visible in news media. This uncertainty is also observable in *Reuters Institute 2018 Digital News Report*, as it links distrust in news media to "high levels of media polarisation, and the perception of undue political influence" (Nic, Fletcher, Kalogeropoulos, Levy, & Nielsen, 2018, p. 9).

Politicians' investment in lies is not a new phenomenon. When one is in the game of power, it is time to do whatever it takes to stay in power. Lying, deceiving, or shifting the truth has always been a part of the politician's game. During Trump's political campaign in 2016 and his presidency, the lies took on a new and trendy mission. They became a propaganda weapon to damage the credibility of journalists (Repucci, Cook, Csaky, & Shahbaz, 2019). Still to this day, the Trump administration uses strategies of extreme populism by fabricating "alternative facts" and attacking critical news media as "fake news," which are claimed to be manufactured by the opposing political parties (Ward, 2018). Furthermore, news media outlets that support Trump administration build parallel realities that support the lies of the government (Kellner, 2018; Ward, 2018). Populist leaders all over the world became a part of this trend. Hungary, Serbia, Turkey, and India are some of the countries that were mentioned in the *Freedom and the Media Report* of Freedom House (Repucci et al., 2019). In this context, the definition of "fake news" faces a significant shift from being the term of disinformation to an expression to mould alternative realities.

*Who is a journalist?*

Another blurry line that causes concerns about trust in the news media and has journalists of the world in a deadlock debate, is between journalism and activism. On February 14, 2018, an expelled student opened fire in his former high school, Marjory Stoneman Douglas High School, killing many people and injuring many more.[9] As the survivors and victims of this mass shooting, students gathered for a march a month later to call for action against gun violence. To talk about the march, the Reliable Sources programme on CNN interviewed Rebecca Schneid live on March 25, 2018. As the student co-editor-in-chief of Marjory Stoneman Douglas High School newspaper, Schneid made a comment on air claiming that "journalism is a form of activism" (Stelter, 2018). This comment started an instant debate on social and mainstream media, mainly among American journalists (Tcholakian, 2018). Josh Kraushaar, politics editor at *National Journal of Washington*, observed Schneid's comment as a misconception on the definition of journalism, and one of the causes of mistrust towards journalists (Kraushaar, 2018). As the debate went on, different opinions on the subject were unravelled. While some journalists, like Lindsay Gellman, were clear on drawing a line between journalism—"using reporting tools to uncover facts, analyse patterns, and publicise those findings"—and activism—"publicly advocating for particular political, legal, social, or other change based on those findings"—some claimed the line to be less visible than it seemed due to having similar effects on the public (Tcholakian, 2018).

This debate took a different turn in the Middle East. In countries, such as Egypt, Qatar, and Turkey, there is a constant battle between the repressive government and journalists, who are trying to seek the truth and defend their freedom (Simon, 2014). Failing to find a place in a distinctly polarised mainstream media, journalists seek to obtain freedom through online communication platforms. In some cases, such as violence in Syria,[10] journalists work side by side with media activists, who provide witness accounts of events (Simon, 2014). A similar act of citizen involvement was also observed throughout Turkey's Gezi Park protests in 2013. While Turkish mainstream media refused to air news about the Gezi protests, active citizens and independent journalists made use of social media platforms to broadcast their own independent news (Tufekci, 2017). Four years after the Gezi protests, the debate on journalism *vs.* activism was brought to the limelight in Turkish news media. Increasing pressures of the government on mainstream media and abstention from investigative journalism brought Turkish journalists to a halt, leaving no other choice but to defend their principles and freedom. Ruşen Çakır (2018), an independent journalist as well as the founding editor and author of mediascope.tv, believes that as it gets harder and harder to practise journalism, journalists are forced to be activists. However, he also believes that journalism should be about reporting news of activists rather than being a part of them. Similarly, Faruk Bildirici (2017), former ombudsman of *Hürriyet Newspaper*, emphasises the very thin line between journalism and activism, and claims that although journalism hosts traits of activism within, these two positions should not be confused with one another. According to Bildirici, in the case of confusion, the journalist becomes the subject of the incident, rather than its pursuer and reporter.

Consequently, although definitions of journalism and activism, as Gellman, Çakır, and Bildirici claim, may differ from one another, the line in between is a contextually varying one. Just as demonstrated above, in countries where mainstream news media are mainly controlled by the government, the definition of a journalist may borrow defensive traits of an activist in order to survive. The aforementioned cases also help to see that there is a clear transformation regarding how news and information work in social media, and formerly established norms and practices of journalism fall insufficient and outdated in such a connected and collaborative media ecosystem (Castellon & Jaramillo, 2011; Hermida, 2012; Spyridou & Veglis, 2016). Advanced mobile devices and globally connected social media platforms provide everyone the authority to access or publish any kind of news. This access also allows horizontal communication between the mainstream media (top-down) and participatory culture (bottom-up). This unregulated space is where definitions of authority and authorship in journalism are called into question (Ciancia & Mattei, 2018). Journalism's formerly closed professional culture and system of editorial control are no longer a feasible operational model for today's openly connected and untamed media environment (Hermida, 2012). This is mainly because the way "news and information are gathered, produced, and disseminated has been profoundly altered" (Gambarato & Tarcia, 2017, p. 4). New stakeholders growingly emerge in the news production and distribution arena, such as news bloggers and citizen journalists. The power of news organisations and journalists slowly decentralises, and professional boundaries and purpose are called into question (Bossio, 2017; Fisher, 2018).

## Who is the news audience?

Instantaneous and global communication among individuals through social media networks provides an environment where people can actively be involved in the "observation, selection, filtering, distribution, and interpretation of events" (Hermida, 2012, p. 309). Nowadays, every citizen with a smartphone and an internet connection can document an event that is witnessed on site and share it globally through various social media platforms (Phillips, 2014). Citizens become prosumers[11] to provide crowdsourcing material to news organisations. This was the case on January 15, 2009, when a plane made an emergency landing on the Hudson River in New York City after losing its engine power.[12] The world became aware of the incident through a photo taken by a man, who was on a ferry close to the crash site. By means of social media, the first images of the incident were distributed globally in an immediate fashion and later used by the mainstream news media. In other words, this time the direction of communication was reversed. Before social media and mobile technology, mainstream media had the lead in distribution of such major incidents; however, now, the connected masses are able to inform each other through instant documenting and sharing of events. Although citizen involvement in news production may have its pros, it may also have its cons. One of the major downsides involves enabling false information to be distributed without a verification process (Bossio, 2017). Just as it happened after April 15, 2013. After the Boston Bombings, mounting speculations on Reddit gave way to an unfortunate witch hunt that accused and targeted innocent people as the bomber. In such cases, one can acknowledge how easily the online environment can turn into chaos and warzone when a single person holds the wrong end of the stick. Unregulated distribution of false information on news websites, blogs, and social media platforms makes it harder to picture a clear path of solution for issues related to safety and trust.

Audience engagement in news production, from another perspective, is the spice that is carefully added to the industry's business model. The audiences' orientation towards personalised news platforms is forcing the news organisations to rethink the old business models that relied solely on advertising (Batsell, 2015; Phillips, 2014). Inviting readers into the news-making process and building a community are slowly being integrated into existing business models to gain new subscriptions and maintain the existing ones. *The Guardian*'s 2012 kick-off campaign on open journalism is one of the cases that clearly indicates this transformation (Sweney, 2012). Through the campaign, *The Guardian* opens up its doors to the readers and invites them to a conversation where they can share ideas and opinions and even pick the topic of news to be covered. However, engaging the audience is not an easy task. As Jake Batsell (2015) emphasises in *Engaged Journalism*, it takes a whole lot of tasks to make the audience feel engaged in the process:

> But while engagement certainly means convincing readers to pay for indispensable journalism, it also means convening the audience in person through events, festivals, and meetups. It means leveraging social media to create conversation, crowdsourcing, and community. It means relentlessly targeting journalism to the specific audience being served, especially if the common denominator for members of that audience is geography or a topical niche. It means empowering the audience with interactive news products such as databases, quizzes, games, and even coloring books. And it means finding a reliable way to track and measure whether all these efforts are making a difference.
>
> (Batsell, 2015, p. 9)

The conversation between the news organisation and its audience has always been existent (Phillips, 2014). However, the conversation has become deeper and broader with "today's digitally empowered audiences", that "demand a more active role" (Batsell, 2015, p. 76).

The perception of audience engagement takes a different turn in the Middle East and North Africa, where the public use of social media to produce news becomes a necessity. In Turkey's Gezi Park (Tufekci, 2017), or the Arab Spring protests, where mainstream news media presented insufficient or non-existent coverage of the incidents, eyewitness citizens made intensive use of social media platforms (Alexander & Aouragh, 2014; Al-Rawi, 2014). Active citizens recorded incidents of real surrounding events and shared them on social media to shout out to the world, breaking the silence of the mainstream news media. In other words, the citizens became citizen journalists[13] to compensate for the public's right to information, since there was no longer any trust towards the mainstream news providers.

Citizen involvement in journalistic affairs blurred the professional borders between the journalist and the audience. This interfluent affair brought forward manifestation of journalism practices that partly engage citizens in the news-making process (Harcup, 2016a, 2016b; Phillips, 2014). Although there are many more perspectives to this observation, the paragraphs above briefly touch upon only some of them. However, whether the audiences are prosumers, engaged communities, or citizen journalists, all of the cases above point to a mutual process: news as a collective conversation (Domingo & Le Cam, 2015).

*Interfluence of behaviours*

It is clear to say that this collective conversation is made possible with emergent digital network of communication via developing media technologies. The collective network allows previously known hierarchical walls of news production and distribution fall down to let horizontal communication flow among all the actors of the process. Firstly, we are no longer bound to mainstream news media outlets that are thin on the ground. Secondly, we have the freedom to choose our own news of interest therefore we migrate to explore what is newsworthy for us. Lastly, we do not passively consume news anymore, instead we join the conversation and use our interactions as prosumers to influence social change. These behavioural shifts, alongside many other reasons, force us to reconsider new business models for news production, distribution and consumption.

*Reading*

Active, migratory, and connected news audiences are changing the balance of the game. Previously obedient media audiences, who unilaterally consumed the choices of mainstream media, now "have become information hunters and gatherers, taking pleasure in tracking information about things that interest them" (Veglis, 2012, p. 314). In other words, it is no longer the storyteller deciding on the newsworthiness and reading order of the story, but the reader drifting along the components of the story while finding ways to interact with it. A recent study, which observes news consumption behaviour of 40 Russian journalism students, reveals a supportive result to this statement (Vartanova, Cherevko, Tolokonnikova, & Dunas, 2019). In their research, the authors define the following phenomenon as *news consumption depth*:

> when the users searched for information on some event, they often did not confine themselves to visiting a single resource but continued navigation. In some cases the respondents wanted to follow some further developments and in others their interest was captured by some irrelevant headline and they went over to something else.
>
> (Vartanova et al., 2019, p. 22)

As in the case of the 40 Russian journalism students, individuals are now using a variety of media platforms and migrating from one to the other in search of news stories. Contemporary participative and story-driven audience wants to explore the many sides of a news story and, if possible, dig deeper into its characters, context, or storyline. Therefore, the expectation is rather a storyworld experience that consists of an immersive storytelling that expands throughout numerous online or offline media channels.

## Storytelling

An infinite amount of good- or bad-quality factual or fake news can be found on countless media channels online. Day and night, we can reach instant information on news from local to global. Such a fast, extensive, and diverse access to news enables limitless storytelling paths to a news story. Therefore, "imposing different degrees of importance for what is being reported" becomes a harder task to accomplish in online news environment (Júnior, 2013, p. 155). Consequently, since the debates of web journalism have been on the scholarly research menu, meaning and function of newsworthiness are pondered on alongside reconsiderations of news storytelling structures (Canavilhas, 2006; Júnior, 2013). Deciding on which information is newsworthy and in which order it should appear in the news story is what inverted pyramid storytelling structure stands for, which is still globally applied in conventional journalism practices (Randall, 2016). However, news production and distribution are no longer limited to a time of printing or broadcasting and borders of a TV screen or a paper. The digital medium imposes rather "a horizontal structure so the user could make his/her own particular path in the content presented, focusing on what interests him/her and not on what was given by an editor as the most important" (Júnior, 2013, p. 155).

Through the years, scholars have proposed different news writing structures that gradually evolve as they are influenced by shifting audience reading patterns. From the inverted pyramid[14] to Canavilhas' (2006) tumbled pyramid,[15] Júnior's (2013) inclusive opened monads model,[16] and Nogueira and Túñez-López's (2019) circular communication flow theory,[17] linear storytelling patterns transform into nonlinear storytelling practices in journalism (Lovato, 2018). These proposed horizontal storytelling structures represent a news environment where all news content is scattered across multiple online or offline, mainstream or non-mainstream news media channels. While the directionless distribution of news brings forward the most commonly talked about problems on news quality, accuracy, and accountability in journalism, it also enables the audience to experience news as an immersive journey.

*Consuming*

In the mesh network of news, the audience is more frequently informed and more emotionally involved. As it was in the case of *Charlie Hebdo* terrorist attacks in France, which occurred in January 2015. People of France and the rest of the world watched the incident unravel as it was concurrently reported. While some viewers passively consumed the news in shock, some took action as they actively interacted by sharing, commenting, investigating, and even forming active crowds on social network platforms. One of the most memorable crowds of the incident perhaps belongs to the "Je Suis Charlie" movement. It was only an image of words that was posted by Joachim Roncin on his Twitter account that went viral in a short period of time (Groll, 2015). Crowds gathered under one slogan on the streets of Paris and social networks around the world "as a gesture of solidarity, resistance, and cathartic reply to violence" (Groll, 2015, para. 6). As observed in this example, social media technologies enable the audience to interact with news events more intimately than ever. Yesterday's passive news consumer now has the voice to take action in the form of large virtual crowds (Friedrichsen & Kamalipour, 2017).

Sometimes these crowds gather around news sources in the form of micro audiences who mainly consume news that focuses on their area of interest (Batsell, 2015, p. 64). Beat journalism perhaps presents a viable environment for these micro audiences to be clearly observed (Batsell, 2015, p. 64). As trust in the news media and, in some cases, access to news become a battle, consumers seek a reliable journalist to loyally follow, who serves as "a trusted filter, guiding and directing the audience to relevant coverage or information" (Batsell, 2015, p. 64). In extreme cases, such as in Turkey, while biased mainstream news media avoids covering news on major political court cases, beat journalists use online news platforms and social media to inform the public solely about these updates within the courthouses. In these specialised news spaces, digital communities interact among themselves and with the journalist, that may later spark actions for social change.

*Interfluence of governance*

There is a global struggle among investigative journalists in being the watchdogs of governmental institutions. Fundamentally, a journalist's task is to collect, analyse, and distribute information to society (Revers, 2017). However, this task entails a significant purpose for a democratic society. In times of societal and governmental decision-making, unbiased news is crucial for the citizens to make informed decisions. Unfortunately, the issue of press freedom is gradually becoming one of the most problematic concerns of contemporary global media environment. The *Freedom House Report* on press freedom and media explains this decline in terms of legal, political, and economic factors (Repucci et al., 2019).

In such an oppressive and limited workspace, a journalist is left to make an important decision: Does one fear losing a job and try to maintain precarity of employment by doing what the authority wants or try to create the circumstances in which one can liberate from censorship and economic constraints (Phillips, 2014). A journalist's freedom from commercial and political constraints would entail editorial independence from related companies and the government (Phillips, 2014). According to the media ethicist Stephen J. A. Ward (2018), conceiving that independence for democracy requires even more:

> Rescuing democracy will require that journalists reconceive their role in society. It will require the articulation of new ethical norms and practices. It will require concrete action. Journalists, in collaboration with other democratic agencies, need to join common cause to detox a polluted public sphere.
>
> (Ward, 2018, p. 3)

What needs an emphasis in this quote is that the battle for press freedom and democracy is only winnable when there are more parties involved working collaboratively. This unity requires "the involvement of those who are outside as well as those who are inside the profession" (Phillips, 2014, p. 79).

The internet age has complicated the position of the journalist by giving institutional actors and citizens "discursive authority" through online platforms (Revers, 2017, p. 5). However, the internet, in this scenario, imitates a double-edged sword, because contemporary online network distribution and crowdfunding infrastructures can also offer means to achieve complete journalistic autonomy. Technological means that an individual journalist would need to reach a wide audience is no longer only in the hands of mainstream media organisations. Mobile communication devices and online broadcast platforms enable an individual journalist to record and release news content from anywhere, at any time to a global audience. On the financial side of it, some self-governed journalism business models—e.g. Through the Cracks (Johnson et al., n.d.), Bongkar (Tempo, 2018), Crikey Digs (Birchall, 2018)—are known to use crowdfunding platforms, such as

Patreon and Kickstarter, to sustain journalistic practice through the donation of the public. The crowdfunding system is also one of the internet's opportunities for the participatory public to be more involved in the news-making process (Friedrichsen & Kamalipour, 2017).

There is a global search for non-partisan and methodologically objective news outlets. The internet age and media convergence are golden opportunities for journalists, who want to do their jobs independently from any governmental institution, political party, organisation, or company. However, this golden opportunity has yet to be discovered. Online news-broadcasting platforms, interactive news audience spaces, and crowdfunding infrastructures are opportunities that are still in the experimentation stage for news makers. Finding a reliable business model for independent journalism initiatives is still a matter of debate. The rest of this chapter takes this issue to a specific geography. It outlines the recent political context of and rising pressure towards journalism practice in Turkey, and the emergence of independent journalism initiatives against this political pressure.

## Mainstream news media in Turkey

Since the beginning of the 2000s, Turkey has been under the ruling of the Justice and Development Party (AKP), who played a major role in the construction of a "New Turkey", which hosts authoritarian, pragmatist, and reactive spirit (Yılmaz, 2018). Ruling New Turkey under a populist regime, the AKP continues to homogenise its society by fear and alienation through mainstream media outlets (Erçetin, 2019). Meanwhile, journalists and the public face violations of ethics and human rights while practicing their freedom of expression and right to information. In countries such as Turkey, where safety of both of these practices cannot be ensured, journalists are constantly left unsupported and in danger (İnceoğlu & Filibeli, 2018).

One of the main reasons behind Turkey's declining news media support for freedom of expression and right to information, hence right to democracy, is the absence of pluralism (İnceoğlu & Filibeli, 2018). The media ownership structure of Turkey has been a lengthy and deeply discussed subject by scholars to understand the relationship between media, ideology, and power (Ethical Journalism Network, 2014; Filibeli & İnceoğlu, 2018; Kurban & Sözeri, 2012; Sözeri, 2017b; Tunç, 2018; "Turkish Media Ownership Network," 2017, "Who owns the media in Turkey," 2016). The Turkish media ownership network is polluted by "conglomerates with energy, construction or mining interests, all sectors heavily dependent on government business" (Ethical Journalism

Network, 2014, p. 15). This network allows the AKP to pull the strings of Turkish media with almost full control.[18] What is at stake under such a controlled and homogenised media ownership structure is free, independent, and diverse opinions that allow criticism of people in power. Similar concerns are also visible on the global scale, raising the need to dig out these buried ownership engagements. The Media Ownership Monitor (MOM) is an initiative that solely serves this purpose. Launched by the German wing of Reporters Without Borders, the initiative investigates media pluralism in developing countries such as Albania, Argentina, Egypt, India, Philippines, and Ukraine (Reporters Without Borders, 2015). It serves as a mapping project that displays an open-to-public and up-to-date database of mass media owners. The project aims at painting a transparent media ownership picture for the public to see who actually owns the media and who influences their opinion ("Who owns the media in Turkey," 2016). In 2016, Turkey entered the list of countries to be investigated by MOM (Akgül, 2016). Media Ownership Monitor Turkey has an ongoing and growing set of data maps and infographics that are updated regularly to make the public aware of constant partnerships between media oligarchs and the governmental institutions ("Who owns the media in Turkey," 2016).

### Distrust, polarisation, and self-censorship

The AKP's control over institutions also brings about high polarisation that paints a black-and-white interplay between pro- and anti-government media. The most recent *Turkey Supplementary Report* of *Reuters Institute Digital News Report* indicates that trust and distrust in Turkish news media are almost exactly the same (Yanatma, 2018). This similarity is one of the clear pictures of how polarised the news media and Turkish society is. Additionally, since the middle of the 1980s, major media companies in Turkey do not employ journalists who are members of a journalists' union. This requirement limits journalists to either consider deunionisation or consent to low paying jobs. In an extremely polarised media environment with no support from the country's legal system, the journalist is solely left with his/her ethical choices (İnceoğlu & Filibeli, 2018; Tunç, 2018). Correspondingly, the journalist is forced to take sides, which falls contrary to professional ethics.

In such a situation that relies on personal ethics, journalists, who do not want to lose their jobs, turn to self-censorship and in some cases, point to their colleagues as targets of scrutiny (Ethical Journalism

Network, 2014; Filibeli & İnceoğlu, 2018; Sözeri, 2017a). In an interview he gave in 2016, Niyazi Dalyancı, the Deputy Secretary-General of the Turkish Journalists' Association, stated his concern as follows:

> I have never seen such [a] state of vileness in my professional life. The journalists today are reporting on their fellow journalists, setting them up to get arrested. I think the profession has hit bottom in terms of ethics and morals. Journalists are to blame for the situation.
>
> (Tunç, 2018, p. 155)

Two years later, in December 2018, a new clause was added to the legislation of press cards. This clause stated that "engaging in acts that are in conflict with national security and public order or having developed a habit of engaging in such activity" would result in the cancelation of a journalist's press card, in other words, work permit (Susma, 2019, p. 73). What this legislation means is that any investigation, social media post, or a news article that went against the order of the government could be the end of a journalist's career. Such a threat shows how much legal power the political establishment has over media companies and journalists, resulting in major political incidents against the government not showing up in mainstream news channels[19] or journalists deliberately reframing news to make up to the government to stay out of trouble. Media ownership and the legal system that is dominated by the government "has created a pool of self-interest for politicians and business leaders, and which in turn compromises ethical journalism" (Ethical Journalism Network, 2014, p. 3).

### *The salty price of self-expression and thought*

Turkey's battle with press freedom, freedom of expression and thought goes back a long way. However, the recent political events have stirred the pot to such an extent that the metaphorical use of the word "battle" in the former sentence is now a battle in the real sense. The Gezi Park protests in 2013 and the coup attempt in 2016 mark a dark time for the mainstream news media companies and journalists, during and in the aftermath. The AKP, as the ruling party during both incidents, has shown that attempting criticism over its regime comes with a price. During the Gezi Park protests, more than 60 journalists lost their jobs and afterwards this number increased to around 300 (Filibeli & İnceoğlu, 2018; Freedom House, 2014). Journalists are imprisoned under antiterrorism laws and there are still ongoing lawsuits against media officials, journalists, and nongovernmental organisation workers. While the AKP puts a spin on the purpose of the Gezi Park protests to reconfigure the news media structure, the critical voices in the mainstream were silenced one by one.

Three years into this upheaval, another earthquake hit the Turkish news media scene with a coup attempt by a US-based Islamic cleric in July 2016. Then Prime Minister Erdoğan, who likened the coup attempt to cancer cells metastasised in the body, applied *chemotherapy*[20] to the sectors he deemed necessary. Around 150 media outlets were shut down and the surviving ones were taken over by pro-government conglomerates (Freedom House, 2019; Reporters Without Borders, 2019). As media pluralism gradually faded away, professional journalists were targeted as traitors by their colleagues, put in jail for more than a year pre-trial, and later sentenced for a long period of time or even a lifetime. According to the *BIA Media Monitoring Report* (2019), during April, May, and June 2019, 19 TV programmes were censored by the Radio and Television Supreme Council (RTÜK), 30 journalists lost their jobs, 213 journalists stood trial, 14 journalists were detained, 10 journalists were assaulted, 70 journalists and media representatives faced 493 years in prison, 3 journalists almost died, and 7 journalists stood trial for insulting the Prime Minister. In addition to these numbers, the online channels of expression are also under governmental attack. There are increasing instances of website censorship, such as the inaccessibility of Wikipedia since April 2017 (for two years and counting), and the passing of a new law that allows RTÜK to control online broadcasting platforms, such as Netflix (Yıldız, 2019).

These cases, numbers, and reports are necessary details to understand the serious depth of legal, ethical, and political situation the journalists of Turkey are trapped in. The government's high walls around mainstream news media outlets and the legal system keep free thought and expression out of the equation, leaving the society shorn of truth, trust, and democratic action, in other words, gradually cracking the foundations and shaking the pillars of democracy.

### Politics of desire for an alternative democratic society

Within all this darkness, the existence of an online digital environment offers alternative channels for diverse voices to be heard. After facing the hardship, many journalism professionals and citizens migrated towards online media outlets, which the government cannot fully control. There are numerous journalists, such as Can Dündar, who were forced to leave the country and continue to make their voices heard through independent news broadcasts abroad (Repucci et al., 2019). New types of social media-based news agency networks formed, such as dokuz8HABER (2014), where citizens collaborate with professional journalists and voluntarily work on bringing local and global news information to the public. What is clear to see is that under this political pressure and polarisation, people from different backgrounds and professions, who are trying to fight for freedom and peace, are resisting in unity. Society is searching for alternative ways to bring back the notion of democracy in Turkey. Zafer Yılmaz (2018, p. 15), in his book about the spirit of New Turkey, describes this perspective of unity through the *politics of desire*, a term influenced by the work of Deleuze and Guattari (1972/1983). The politics of desire points to a collective social production and actions. According to Deleuze and Guattari (1972/1983), desire is a strategic resource for reform and freedom, new lifestyles and ways of thinking, and it needs to be produced. It refers to a reform, but this reform does not happen through actions of destroying, forgetting or throwing away. It happens through making additions to the scenario, taking strategies from other places and making unexpected changes (Goodchild, 1996). In other words, the reform that is described by Deleuze and Guattari (1972/1983) happens by entering into social relations instead of liberating from social expectations. Coming back to Yılmaz's (2018) perspective, he adapts the understanding of the politics of desire as a favourable approach to overcome the oppressed system of New Turkey. According to Yılmaz, the emerging politics that stem out of the constituent power of collaboration, creativity of freedom, joint action of citizenship, and partnership between all living creatures should be integrated with a micro-politics—politics of desire—that questions all authorities and liberates the spirit of New Turkey (2018, p. 15). The following section describes the emergence of independent journalism initiatives, which aim at building an alternative democratic society by standing in collaboration against the oppressive power, asking all sorts of questions, and liberating the voice of the oppressed.

## Independent journalism initiatives in Turkey

What gradually faded away in Turkey's mainstream news media is having the right to ask questions to reveal the facts about governmental affairs. In time, investigative journalism perhaps took the hardest blow among all the other journalism approaches. The government may have thrown the biggest punches, but that was not the only reason behind this fall. In a face-to-face conversation, Aslı Tunç, a media professor at

Istanbul Bilgi University, stated that this gradual depreciation did not just happen overnight and there were many factors behind it. However, according to Tunç, one of the obvious factors was the lack of investment in good journalism. She was talking about an environment where hard-working/fact-hunting journalists earned so much less money and appreciation than celebrated opinion-makers/columnists. Moreover, she indicated that the investment was also mainly made for the technological infrastructure of mass media outlets. In other words, the glossy printing press was favoured against journalists, who were focused on producing good-quality news content.

With all of the obstructive factors, practicing journalism within the existent mainstream news media system has become almost impossible in Turkey. Although independent initiatives of journalism did exist before the ultimate deterioration of mainstream news media, after the Gezi Park protests in 2013 and the failed coup incident in 2016, these initiatives—Platform24, Ünsal Ünlü, Bianet, Medyascope, Diken, Artı Gerçek, Journo—multiplied in number and elevated in voice.

### *The resistance*

Most of these independent initiatives share a common mission: protect the public's right to information and truth; defend democracy, fundamental freedoms, and secularism; restore the reputation and dignity of the journalism profession; establish a civil, independent, free, and pluralistic media environment; support editorial independence, press freedom, and quality journalism; discover what the digital media network can offer to journalism practice in the process; create a hub for the young reporters; and bring solidarity among journalists that they cannot find in corporate media outlets. However, they all approach this mission from different angles of focus, project structures, and support systems. While some focus on new media broadcasting, emerging news production technologies, and lives of journalists, some follow this mission in pursuit of minority rights. Some initiatives bring professional journalists together with various independent organisations, while others prefer to work under their own steam, maintaining full independence. Financially, some are supported by independent organisations, while others continue to exist with advertising revenue and public donations through crowdfunding. In most cases, these financial support structures are transparently presented in detail. The diversity of focus, structure, and support among these independent initiatives are explained more clearly in Chapter 4, where some of these initiatives are analysed in detail.

## Paddle your own canoe

When independent journalism initiatives are taken into consideration, questions arise in one's mind. One of these questions is what does the term *independence* mean in this mission? What methods can be applied to ensure this independence, when we know these initiatives require financial support from external structures to survive? Issues of independence and transparency have always been discussed in journalism studies and practice. However, it is crucial to observe how newly emerging digital news media approaches and practices the notion of independence, in order to ensure that the concept of independent journalism mentioned in this book is semantically in place.

What these initiatives define as independent journalism is a practice that abstains from being the voice of a political party, company, organisation, or a religious cult. Suffering a never-ending abuse from demanding commercial industry and government propaganda scenarios, these initiatives are experimenting with new business models, where they can paddle their own canoe and maximise their distance of bias in the process. These experiments are only available because contemporary online news and social network platforms enable them to be. However, as every project requires a budget, these initiatives also need to depend on external financial support for sustainability. In this circumstance, the notion of *independence* arouses a suspicion, which these initiatives need to break with transparency. Case in point, Platform24 works with various external organisations, such as the EU and United Nations Educational, Scientific, and Cultural Organization (UNESCO), for specific projects. For proof of independence from these organisations, their website announces that "in the interests of full transparency and disclosure P24 will submit its financial accounts to a full and publicly available audit, undertaken by the firm of KPMG", which is an audit, tax and consulting services provider (Platform24, 2014b). Another case in point is Journo. The initiative is owned by the Journalists' Union of Turkey (TGS) and maintains its editorial independence from the union (Journo, 2017). It also receives support from a programme funded by the European Union. The programme budget is transparently revealed on the initiative's website.

## The alternative or the new mainstream?

In pursuit of independence and media pluralism, these independent journalism initiatives also brought about a definitional debate between mainstream and alternative media within the context of

Turkey. In its early emergence, alternative media used to be defined as a binary opposition to mainstream or legacy media. It was defined as an alternative space where audiences become active participants of democratic society through a diverse range of content (Hamilton, 2000). This perspective was clear when mainstream media content and practices was yet to merge with online social platforms, or vice versa (Kenix, 2011). The convergence of communication technologies made it all the more confusing to reposition the term *alternative* when all the media platforms, the content, and ownership structures meld into one another, leaving no difference to define one in contrast to the other (Harcup, 2005; Holt, Figenschou, & Frischlich, 2019; Kenix, 2011). Contemporary hybrid media systems (Chadwick, 2017) navigate this definitional debate between alternative and legacy media towards "a continuum rather than as absolutely opposed categories" (Holt et al., 2019, p. 2). In a recent article titled *Key Dimensions of Alternative News Media*, Holt, Figenschou, and Frischlich (2019) describe the baffling nature of defining the position of a medium in such a hybrid environment:

> Beyond the perceived counter-hegemonic aim, [...], multiple combinations of alternativeness are possible, and often probable, although not necessary. How and on what level the counter-hegemonic agenda is played out is a question for empirical, contextualised research. In essence, the more a given medium differs from the mainstream, the more likely it is that it is perceived as an alternative serving the function of remedying some ill or compensating for deficits associated with the mainstream.
>
> (2019, p. 6)

Contextual factors may change how mainstream and alternative notions of media are perceived. As also touched very briefly in the same article, in the context of Turkey, these two media spheres are, perhaps, changing places with each other. Speaking in an interview, Ali Duran Topuz, Editor-in-Chief of the independent journalism platform Gazete Duvar, explains his version of how this interchange is possible as follows:

> The new media means the transformation of the medium. This also means the transformation of human relations, humans and political relations. The old media had a very defined, very clear link with capital and politics. We could easily measure the location, characteristics and boundaries of the mainstream and the alternative. Now we see an area where there are countless possibilities

but none of these things can be measured. When we add the political situation in our country [to this equation], we define the area where on the one hand it is very pessimistic and on the other hand there are opportunities and problems in which the efforts of one person can be very effective.

(Duvar, 2018, para. 4)

Joining Topuz in his perspective is Ünsal Ünlü, a former mainstream radio and television journalist who worked in various levels of news media, and one of the independently working journalists of today. Ünlü, in his recent talk at the Gazeteciler Cemiyeti Basın Evi (Press House of Journalists' Association), claims that the mainstream media in Turkey has now become the alternative. According to Ünlü, the independent initiatives' success in becoming the new force of pursuit to the masses enables them to say, "we are not alternatives, we are the television itself" (24 Saat, 2019). Ruşen Çakır, journalist, author and founder of the independent journalism initiative Medyascope, joins the argument by emphasising that Medyascope could be the mainstream and appeal to everyone, claiming that they are not opposites or alternatives and they don't hold an activist position (Tunç, 2016). In light of the changes in political regime that influence the definition of mainstream media in Turkey, it is, perhaps, sound to question whether the legacy media, that was formerly defined as the mainstream, has transformed into an alternative, subversive, or even transgressive entity (Holt et al., 2019). Being aware of this contextually complex interchange is pivotal in understanding the position of the independent journalism initiatives and the complexity of the battle they pursue against the oppressors in claiming the power of media with the support of a democratic society.

### *Expanding to audiences*

Winning this media power battle requires a wide range of participants. Reaching a large audience is not an easy task. As the *Reuters Institute Digital News Report of Turkey* indicates, online media has become the primary source of news for all ages of the Turkish society with a weekly reach of 87% (Yanatma, 2018). The online digital network provides the infrastructure to distribute content to a global audience and build an environment for interaction; however, production and distribution of this content require careful planning of structure, organisation, and management. As each independent journalism initiative has its own specific focus, each has its own content distribution strategies to reach their ideal audience. For instance, Platform24 not only practises investigative journalism but also organises training workshops for future journalists and partners with other news initiatives on specific projects, also conducts national and international projects to bring "issues of media integrity to public attention" (Platform24, 2014a). It expands these projects across news websites, reports, lectures, workshops, social media platforms, and other media of access to the masses.

In the absence of mainstream distribution, expanding messages among various media outlets becomes a necessary strategy for any initiative to reach audiences of mixed demographics. Journalists, who are alienated from the legacy media outlets, are on the search to find alternative methods to reach out to the public. New ways of storytelling that encourage interactivity seem pivotal in their independent mission of independence, press freedom, diversity, and most importantly, building a democratic society.

## Notes

1 The idea of transmedia ethos refers to a deeper understanding of transmediality. It suggests the audience's migration across media in pursuit of common beliefs, values, themes, philosophies, and meanings rather than stories (Freeman, 2016, 2018a, 2018b; Freeman & Taylor-Ashfield, 2017).

2 On September 28, 1980, Janet Cooke, who was a journalist of *The Washington Post* at the time, wrote a news article titled *Jimmy's World*. The article told the story of a boy who is an eight-year-old heroin addict living in Southeast Washington. This heart-wrenching story earned Cooke a Pulitzer Prize. The reality checked in when the public wanted to reach out to the little boy for help, but no one could find him. Cooke, unable to provide a solid source for her news story, was publicly disgraced and her Pulitzer Prize was taken back.

3 During the 1990s, it was discovered that Stephen Glass managed to fabricate the articles that were published in the *News Republic Magazine*. In 2003, an American film directed by Billy Ray titled *Shattered Glass* had been released. The film is based on the events that happened up until the truth was uncovered.

4 Michael Finkel's journalism career hit a dead end when he confessed to fabricating the article "Is Youssouf Malé a Slave" published in *New York Times Magazine* in November 18, 2001. The article was about child slavery in West Africa. Unable to find adequate source to back up his story, Finkel composed an imaginary adolescent West African boy in Mali, named Malé, and told his story in convincing detail. In 2015, the true story of Finkel was adapted to an American film directed by Rupert Goold, which was titled *True Story*.

5 As a very recent case, on December 19, 2018, it was announced that Claas Relotius, a successful journalist, has been fabricating news stories for *Der Spiegel*. This incident was uncovered through Relotius' latest article about Trump supporters in Fergus Falls, Minnesota. When two locals of the

area realised the invented representation of their hometown, they posted their findings on a blog. Discovery of further evidence of fabrication in former articles led to death of his career as a journalist.

6 The concept of objectivity in news reporting has been commonly regarded as being absolutely free of bias and neutral. However, Kovach and Rosenstiel (2014) aim to clarify the misunderstanding behind this concept by claiming that subjectivity and bias will always exist in everything we do, but using objective methods of verification—thoroughness, accuracy, fairness, and transparency—can help us come closer to fact-based truth.

7 In January 2017, an article in a UK news website, *Express*, posted the headline "Merkel calls for EU army to defend Europe as relations with UK and USA weaken" (Gutteridge, 2017). The article provided no factual information or reliable source on the issue. The situation snowballed and concerns arose among the public as the headline took over social media. Later on, Merkel denied the claims of such a call and *Express'* article was understood to be just another fake news.

8 In June of 2013, during the Gezi Park protests in Istanbul, Erdoğan, who was then the Prime Minister of Turkey at the time, made a public speech about a woman with a headscarf, who was violently assaulted in Kabataş by Gezi Park protesters. This alleged incident was claimed to be investigated by the government, while pro-government news media outlets ran justifying headlines of the incident without any reliable source. It was a long wait until February of 2014 when a security camera footage of the incident was released to the public, proving that such an incident, in fact, did not happen.

9 Expelled student Nikolas Cruz opened fire to his former schoolmates and teachers on February 14, 2018. Marjory Stoneman Douglas High School in Florida became a massacre ground on that Valentine's Day. Seventeen people were killed, and seventeen others were injured.

10 While international journalists were not allowed to report from Syria, the citizens took over the practice and used social and online network sites, such as *The Syrian Revolution* page, the *Sham Network*, and the *Local Coordination Committees* page (Noueihed, 2018). These websites received videos, which were carefully verified and then shared with international news outlets.

11 The term prosumer is commonly used to describe "an active audience that creates, modifies, and participates in products online" (Jenkins, 2006; Phillips, 2014, p. 89).

12 In 2016, an American film directed by Clint Eastwood titled *Sully: Miracle on the Hudson* had been released. The film portrays the emergency landing of US Airways Flight 1549 on the Hudson River in 2009.

13 Collaborative eyewitness reporting of events has brought forward the concept of citizen journalism (Allan, 2013). However, "journalism" attribute to citizen eyewitness reportage is still in debate due to its "spontaneous, spur-of-the-moment responses, so often motivated by a desire to connect with others" (Allan, 2013, p. 1). Recently, new attempts to change the existing terminology are emerging such as citizen witnessing.

14 The inverted pyramid has mostly been the conventionally ideal structure of writing news stories (Júnior, 2013; Randall, 2016). This structure prioritises newsworthy information and releases it to the reader

upfront. Information that is less newsworthy, is situated at the bottom of the pyramid and it is released to the reader later on. In this perspective, the news reader is able to follow a linear path as the story unravels over the words of the journalist.

15 Canavilhas' tumbled pyramid is a four-levelled structure that liberates the physical constraints of the formerly used inverted pyramid structure. Mimicking the unlimited boundaries of internet, tumbled pyramid allows "the possibility either of following through only one of the available reading axes or of navigating freely across the news" (Canavilhas, 2006, p. 14).

16 Instead of the conventional vertical pyramid model of reading, what Junior proposes is a horizontal model that represents the non-linear reading structure of transmedia news stories, making each fragmented article of a news story as important as the next one (Júnior, 2013).

17 According to Nogueira and Túñez, contemporary communication structures are not hierarchical anymore. Contemporary communication technologies offer multiple connection paths, "with narrative models in various formats and with circular flow structures" (Nogueira & Túñez-López, 2019, p. 965).

18 On July 18, 2019, journalist Yavuz Oğhan broadcasted an interview on his own YouTube channel with the former prime minister of Turkey, Ahmet Davutoğlu. The next day, Oğhan's radio program on RS FM, a radio station controlled by the Russian news agency Sputnik, was cancelled. Editor-in-Chief of Sputnik Turkey, Mahir Boztepe, justified firing Oğhan by saying that Davutoğlu's explanations are not newsworthy, they would not want to be the spreader of his words and that they have previously warned Oğhan not to do the interview (T24, 2019). Soon after, Zafer Arapkirli, who is also known for his critical opinions towards the government and was not afraid to speak out in his radio programs in RS FM, was fired (Diken, 2019).

19 During the Gezi Park protests, major mainstream news media outlets, such as CNN Türk, preferred broadcasting a documentary on penguins, rather than informing the public about what was going on. Public outrage to this censorship has continued in the months or even years to come. CNN Türk's ignorance influenced the #occupygezi movement with street art and graffiti of penguins, wearing tear gas masks or gathering in colonies.

20 The term "chemotherapy" in this sentence is used in a metaphorical sense to match the Turkish Prime Minister's statement.

# References

24 Saat. (2019, June 22). Ünlü: Biz alternatif değiliz, televizyonun kendisiyiz. Retrieved July 27, 2019, from 24SaatGazetesi website: http://www.24saat gazetesi.com/unlu-biz-alternatif-degiliz-televizyonun-kendisiyiz/

Akgül, E. (2016). "Media Ownership Monitor Turkey" project by Bianet, Reporter ohne Grenzen presented at Press Conference. Retrieved August 11, 2019, from Bianet website: https://m.bianet.org/english/media/180053-media-ownership-monitor-turkey-project-by-bianet-reporter-ohne-grenzen-presented-at-press-conference

Alexander, A., & Aouragh, M. (2014). Arab revolutions: Breaking fear | Egypt's unfinished revolution: The role of the media revisited. *International Journal of Communication Systems, 8*, 890–915.

Allan, S. (2013). *Citizen Witnessing: Revisioning Journalism in Times of Crisis.* John Wiley & Sons.

Al-Rawi, A. K. (2014). Arab revolutions: Breaking fear | The Arab spring & online protests in Iraq. *International Journal of Communication Systems, 8*, 916–942.

Batsell, J. (2015). *Engaged Journalism: Connecting with Digitally Empowered News Audiences.* Columbia University Press.

Bianet. (2019, July 23). BIA media monitoring / April-May-June 2019: Good news of 3 months: Constitutional court rulings on "Press Freedom Violation." Retrieved July 25, 2019, from Bianet - Bağımsız İletişim Ağı website: https://bianet.org/english/media/210760-good-news-of-3-months-constitutional-court-rulings-on-press-freedom-violation

Bi̇ldi̇ri̇ci̇, F. (2017, July 10). Gazetecilik ve aktivizm. Retrieved March 19, 2019, from Hürriyet website: http://www.hurriyet.com.tr/yazarlar/faruk-bildirici/gazetecilik-ve-aktivizm-40514815

Birchall, B. (2018). Crikey digs. Retrieved July 20, 2019, from Pozible website: https://www.pozible.com/project/crikey-digs

Bossio, D. (2017). *Journalism and Social Media: Practitioners, Organisations and Institutions.* Springer.

Çakır, R. (2018, November 16). Gazetecilik ve aktivizm. Retrieved March 19, 2019, from rusencakir.com website: http://rusencakir.com/Gazetecilik-ve-aktivizm/6866

Canavilhas, J. (2006). Webjornalismo: Da pirâmide invertida à pirâmide de-itada. *BOCC—Biblioteca Online de Ciências da Comunicação.* Retrieved from http://www.bocc.ubi.pt/~boccmirror/pag/canavilhas-joao-webjornalismo-piramide-invertida.pdf

Carson, A. (2019). *Investigative Journalism, Democracy and the Digital Age.* Routledge.

Castellon, L., & Jaramillo, O. (2011). Digital competencies for journalists. In E. P. Matteo Ciastellardi (Ed.), *Understanding Media, Today: McLuhan in the Era of Convergence Culture* (pp. 293–305). Editorial Universidad Oberta de Catalunya.

Chadwick, A. (2017). *The Hybrid Media System: Politics and Power.* Oxford University Press.

Ciancia, M., & Mattei, M. (2018). Tell me a story, but it should be real!: Design practice in transmedia journalism. In R. R. Gambarato & G. C. Alzamora (Eds.), *Exploring Transmedia Journalism in the Digital Age* (pp. 104–125). IGI Global.

Dethreading. (n.d.). In *YourDictionary.* Retrieved from https://www.yourdictionary.com/dethreading

Deleuze, G., & Guattari, F. (1983). *Anti-Oedipus: Capitalism and Schizophrenia.* University of Minnesota Press. (Original work published 1972)

Diken. (2019, July 21). Yavuz Oğhan: Davutoğlu'nda haber değeri görmeyen kendine gazeteci demesin. Retrieved August 12, 2019, from Diken website:

http://www.diken.com.tr/yavuz-oghan-davutoglunda-haber-degeri-gormeyen-kendine-gazeteci-demesin/

dokuz8HABER. (2014). Home page. Retrieved July 25, 2019, from dokuz8HABER website: https://dokuz8haber.net/kategori/english/

Domingo, D., & Le Cam, F. (2015). Journalism beyond the boundaries: The collective construction of news narratives. In M. Carlson & S. C. Lewis (Eds.), *Boundaries of Journalism* (pp. 137–151). Routledge.

Duvar. (2018, October 24). Mülkiyeliler'de yeni medya konuşuldu. Retrieved July 27, 2019, from Gazete Duvar website: https://www.gazeteduvar.com.tr/gundem/2018/10/24/mulkiyelilerde-yeni-medya-konusuldu/

Erçetin, T. (2019). Bir popülist korku senaryosu altında: "biz ve onlar." In P. U. Semerci & E. Erdoğan (Eds.), *Siyasetteki Gölge Korku* (pp. 189–231). İthaki Yayınları.

Ethical Journalism Network. (2014). *Censorship in The Park: Turkish Media Trapped by Politics and Corruption*. Retrieved from https://ethicaljournalismnetwork.org/wp-content/uploads/2016/08/censorship-in-the-park.pdf

Filibeli, T. E., & İnceoğlu, Y. G. (2018). From political economy of the media to press freedom: Obstacles to the implementation of peace journalism in Turkey. *Conflict & Communication, 17*(1), 1–11.

Fisher, C. (2018). What is meant by "trust" in news media? In A. K. Kim Otto (Ed.), *Trust in Media and Journalism* (pp. 19–38). Springer VS.

Freedom House. (2014). *Democracy in Crisis: Corruption, Media, and Power in Turkey*. Freedom House.

Freedom House. (2019, January 30). Turkey. Retrieved July 24, 2019, from Freedom in The World 2019 website: https://freedomhouse.org/report/freedom-world/2019/turkey

Freeman, M. (2016). Small change – Big difference: Tracking the transmediality of Red Nose Day. *View: Journal of European Television History and Culture, 5*(10), 87–96.

Freeman, M. (2018a). New paths in transmediality as vast narratives. *Reading Contemporary Serial Television Universes*, 9–26. https://doi.org/10.4324/9781315114668-2

Freeman, M. (2018b). Transmedia charity: Constructing the ethos of the BBC's Red Nose Day across media. In M. Freeman & R. R. Gambarato (Eds.), *The Routledge Companion to Transmedia Studies* (pp. 306–313). Routledge.

Freeman, M., & Taylor-Ashfield, C. (2017). "I read comics from a feministic point of view": Conceptualizing the transmedia ethos of the Captain Marvel fan community. *The Journal of Fandom Studies, 5*, 317–335. https://doi.org/10.1386/jfs.5.3.317_1

Friedrichsen, M., & Kamalipour, Y. R. (2017). *Digital Transformation in Journalism and News Media*. Springer.

Gambarato, R. R., & Tarcia, L. P. T. (2017). Transmedia strategies in journalism. *Journalism Studies, 18*(11), 1381–1399.

Gillers, S. (2018). *Journalism under Fire: Protecting the Future of Investigative Reporting*. Columbia University Press.

Goodchild, P. (1996). *Gilles Deleuze and the Question of Philosophy*. Fairleigh Dickinson University Press.

Groll, E. (2015, January 19). Meet the man who put the "Je Suis" in the "Je Suis Charlie." Retrieved July 16, 2019, from Foreign Policy website: https://foreignpolicy.com/2015/01/19/meet-the-man-who-put-the-je-suis-in-the-je-suis-charlie/

Gutteridge, N. (2017, January 13). Merkel calls for EU army to defend Europe as relations with UK and USA weaken. Retrieved July 27, 2019, from Express.co.uk website: https://www.express.co.uk/news/world/753750/Angela-Merkel-Germany-EU-army-Trump-Brexit

Hamilton, J. (2000). Alternative media: Conceptual difficulties, critical possibilities. *Journal of Communication Inquiry, 24*, 357–378. https://doi.org/10.1177/0196859900024004002

Hanitzsch, T., Hanusch, F., Ramaprasad, J., & de Beer, A. S. (2019). *Worlds of Journalism: Journalistic Cultures around the Globe.* Columbia University Press.

Happer, C., Hoskins, A., & Merrin, W. (2018). *Trump's Media War.* Springer.

Harcup, T. (2005). "I'm doing this to change the world": Journalism in alternative and mainstream media. *Journalism Studies, 6*, 361–374. https://doi.org/10.1080/14616700500132016

Harcup, T. (2016a). Alternative journalism as monitorial citizenship? *Digital Journalism, 4*, 639–657. https://doi.org/10.1080/21670811.2015.1063077

Harcup, T. (2016b). Asking the readers. *Journalism Practice, 10*, 680–696. https://doi.org/10.1080/17512786.2015.1054416

Heinrich, A. (2011). *Network Journalism: Journalistic Practice in Interactive Spheres.* Routledge.

Hermida, A. (2012). Social journalism: Exploring how social media is shaping journalism. In E. Siapera & A. Veglis (Eds.), *The Handbook of Global Online Journalism* (pp. 309–328). Wiley-Blackwell.

Hirst, M. (2011). *News 2.0: Can Journalism Survive the Internet?* Allen & Unwin Sydney.

Holt, K., Figenschou, T. U., & Frischlich, L. (2019). Key dimensions of alternative news media. *Digital Journalism*, 1–10. https://doi.org/10.1080/21670811.2019.1625715

İnceoğlu, Y. G., & Filibeli, T. E. (2018). Providing a "new road map" to the obstacles of peace journalism in Turkey. *Journalism "a Peacekeeping Agent" at the Time of Conflict.* https://doi.org/10.1163/9789004386365_003

Jenkins, H. (2006). *Convergence Culture: Where Old and New Media Collide.* NYU Press.

Johnson, K., Helm, W., Moreno, R., Hutsell, M., Montoya, S., Hume, K., ... Basilaia, E. (n.d.). Through the cracks: Crowdfunding in journalism. Retrieved July 21, 2019, from http://throughcracks.com/

Journo. (2017, March 7). Hakkımızda. Retrieved July 26, 2019, from Journo website: https://journo.com.tr/hakkimizda

Júnior, C. P. (2013). Opened monads: The evolution of a concept. *Brazilian Journalism Research.* Retrieved from http://bjr.sbpjor.org.br/bjr/article/view/570

Kellner, D. (2018). Donald Trump and the politics of lying. In M. A. Peters, S. Rider, M. Hyvönen, & T. Besley (Eds.), *Post-Truth, Fake News: Viral Modernity & Higher Education* (pp. 89–100). Singapore: Springer Singapore.

Kenix, L. J. (2011). *Alternative and Mainstream Media: The Converging Spectrum*. A&C Black.

Kovach, B., & Rosenstiel, T. (2014). *The Elements of Journalism: What Newspeople Should Know and the Public Should Expect*. Three Rivers Press.

Kraushaar, J. (2018, March 26). Josh Kraushaar on Twitter. Retrieved March 16, 2019, from Twitter website: https://twitter.com/HotlineJosh/status/978019910625452034

Kurban, D., & Sözeri, C. (2012). Caught in the wheels of power. *TESEV Democratization Program Media Studies Series, 3.* Retrieved from http://insanhaklarisavunuculari.org/dokumantasyon/files/original/a0ced433bacb9c369087b5c95346ef10.pdf

Lovato, A. (2018). The transmedia script for nonfictional narratives. In *Exploring Transmedia Journalism in the Digital Age* (pp. 235–252). IGI Global.

Nic, N., Fletcher, R., Kalogeropoulos, A., Levy, D. A. L., & Nielsen, R. K. (2018). *Reuters Institute Digital News Report 2018*. Reuters Institute for the Study of Journalism.

Nogueira, A. G. F., & Túñez-López, M. (2019). Multidimensional and multidirectional journalistic narrative: From tumbled pyramid to circular communication. *Advances in Intelligent Systems and Computing*, 965–974. https://doi.org/10.1007/978-3-030-11890-7_90

Noueihed, W. (2018). Reading the Arab revolutions: Authoritarianism and the implications of change. *AlMuntaqa*, 1, 102. https://doi.org/10.31430/almuntaqa.1.2.0102

Peters, M. A., Rider, S., Hyvönen, M., & Besley, T. (2018). *Post-Truth, Fake News: Viral Modernity & Higher Education*. Springer.

Phillips, A. (2014). *Journalism in Context: Practice and Theory for the Digital Age*. Routledge.

Platform24. (2014a, January 24). About us. Retrieved July 27, 2019, from Platform24 website: http://platform24.org/en/about-us

Platform24. (2014b, January 24). We work with. Retrieved July 26, 2019, from Platform24 website: http://platform24.org/en/we-work-with

Price, S. (2019). *Journalism, Power and Investigation: Global and Activist Perspectives*. Routledge.

Randall, D. (2016). *The Universal Journalist – Fifth Edition* (5th ed.). Pluto Press.

Reporters Without Borders. (2015). FAQ. Retrieved August 12, 2019, from Media Ownership Monitor website: http://www.mom-rsf.org/en/about/faq/

Reporters Without Borders. (2019, April 4). Turkey: Massive purge. Retrieved July 24, 2019, from RSF website: https://rsf.org/en/turkey

Repucci, S., Cook, S., Csaky, Z., & Shahbaz, A. (2019). *Freedom and the Media 2019: A Downward Spiral*. Freedom House.

Revers, M. (2017). *Contemporary Journalism in the US and Germany: Agents of Accountability*. Springer.

Simon, J. (2014). *The New Censorship: Inside the Global Battle for Media Freedom*. Columbia University Press.

Sözeri, C. (2017a). *Ethics in the News - Turkey: After an Attempted Coup the Journalists' Nightmare.* Retrieved from Ethical Journalism Network website: https://ethicaljournalismnetwork.org/resources/publications/ethics-in-the-news/turkey

Sözeri, C. (2017b). Turkey: Sacrificing credibility for economic expediency and partisanship. In T. Eberwein, S. Fengler, & M. Karmasin (Eds.), *The European Handbook of Media Accountability* (pp. 268–276). Routledge.

Spyridou, L. P., & Veglis, A. (2016). Convergence and the changing labor of journalism: Towards the "super journalist" paradigm. In A. Lugmayr & C. Dal Zotto (Eds.), *Media Convergence Handbook – Vol. 1. Media Business and Innovation* (pp. 99–116). Springer, Berlin, Heidelberg.

Stelter, B. (2018, March 27). Journalism and activism: This "Reliable Sources" segment sparked a debate. Retrieved March 16, 2019, from CNNMoney website: https://money.cnn.com/2018/03/27/media/journalism-activism-reliable-sources/index.html

Susma. (2019). *Censorship and Self-Censorship in Turkey: December 2017 - December 2018.* Punto24 Platform for Independent Journalism.

Sweney, M. (2012, February 29). Guardian TV ad kicks off "open journalism" campaign. Retrieved April 6, 2019, from the Guardian website: http://www.theguardian.com/media/2012/feb/29/guardian-tv-ad-open-journalism

T24. (2019, July 21). Yavuz Oğhan: Davutoğlu'nun söyleyeceklerinde haber değeri görmeyecek olan kendisine gazeteci demesin. Retrieved August 12, 2019, from T24 website: https://t24.com.tr/haber/yavuz-oghan-davutoglu-nun-soyleyeceklerinde-haber-degeri-gormeyecek-olan-kendisine-gazeteci-demesin, 831580

Tcholakian, D. (2018, March 29). Is journalism a form of activism? Retrieved March 16, 2019, from Longreads website: https://longreads.com/2018/03/29/is-journalism-a-form-of-activism/

Tempo. (2018, January 8). Tempo news: Crowdfunding journalism, new way to get powerful. Retrieved July 21, 2019, from Tempo.co website: https://en.tempo.co/read/914645/tempo-news-crowdfunding-journalism-new-way-to-get-powerful

Tufekci, Z. (2017). *Twitter and Tear Gas: The Power and Fragility of Networked Protest.* Yale University Press.

Tunç, A. (2016, January 10). Başka bir ana akım medya mümkün mü? Retrieved July 27, 2019, from P24 Blog website: http://p24blog.org/yazarlar/1292/baska-bir-ana-akim-medya-mumkun-mu-

Tunç, A. (2018). All is flux: A hybrid media approach to macro-analysis of the Turkish media. *Middle East Critique, 27*(2), 141–159.

Turkish Media Ownership Network (2017). Network of Dispossession. Retrieved July 23, 2019, from http://mulksuzlestirme.org/turkiye-medya-sahipleri-agi/

Vartanova, E., Cherevko, T., Tolokonnikova, A., & Dunas, D. (2019). Changing patterns of digital news consumption among Russian journalism students. *World of Media. Journal of Russian Media and Journalism Studies, 1*(1), 7–30.

Veglis, A. (2012). From cross media to transmedia reporting in newspaper articles. *Pub Res Q, 28*(4), 313–324.

Wahl-Jorgensen, K., & Hanitzsch, T. (2019). *The Handbook of Journalism Studies*. Routledge.

Ward, S. J. A. (2018). *Ethical Journalism in a Populist Age: The Democratically Engaged Journalist*. Rowman & Littlefield.

Who owns the media in Turkey (2016). Media Ownership Monitor. Retrieved August 11, 2019, from https://turkey.mom-rsf.org/

Yanatma, S. (2018). *Reuters Institute Digital News Report 2018: Turkey Supplementary Report*. Reuters Institute; University of Oxford.

Yıldız, C. (2019, August 1). RTÜK Üyesi İlhan Taşcı: Netflix'i bol "bip"li izleyeceğimiz günler geliyor. Retrieved August 7, 2019, from T24 website: https://t24.com.tr/video/rtuk-uyesi-ilhan-tasci-netflix-i-bol-bip-li-izleyece gimiz-gunler-geliyor, 20737

Yılmaz, Z. (2018). *Yeni Türkiye'nin ruhu: hınç, tahakküm, muhtaçlaştırma*. İletişim Yayınları.

# 3 Rethreading with transmediality

**Kintsugi**

(n.) an ancient Japanese practice of filling the cracks of a broken pottery with gold or silver lacquer. It is a physical manifestation of resilience that gives a unique value to a depreciated matter.

Chapter 2 laid out some of the reasons why foundation of trust in the news media is shaking globally, cracking the core of democracy even in the most developed societies. Considering our specific geography, Turkey's governmental oppression towards mainstream and online news media deepen these cracks. The idea of a democratic society is broken into pieces as media plurality, freedom of expression, and critical thought gets harder to maintain. That being the case, the art of kintsugi is, perhaps, a proper metaphor to explain why transmediality and other experimental efforts in journalism practice are golden lacquers in between the broken pieces of a democratic society. It is a metaphor fitting to the resilience that is demonstrated by ethical journalists, "who toil in the fields of journalism, upholding their integrity and their public purpose, in a media world seemingly gone mad" (Ward, 2018, sec. Dedication).

It would not be far-fetched to question whether the dethreading of journalism practice from multiple angles lay the groundwork for feasibility and, perhaps, necessity of transmediality in news industry. In this regard, this chapter sets off to discover conceptual bridges between independent journalism and transmedia journalism. But how does the notion of transmediality, among other efforts, serve as a golden string to rethread the broken trust, transparency, independence, and plurality of news media in countries like Turkey? Answer to this question entails the understanding of (1) how transmedia narratives manifest in journalism practices, (2) how the notion of transmedia ethos plays a part in culturally uniting an interactive society, and (3) how the initiatives of independent journalism in Turkey relate to the overall structural and cultural aspects of transmediality. This chapter dwells upon these areas to highlight the vital role of transmediality in journalism, especially from the fresh perspective of Turkey. The resulting highlights also serve as indicators for the methodological framework of this investigation. Chapter 4 utilises the principles, concepts, and relations, discussed in this chapter, to demonstrate the role of transmediality on independent journalism cases in Turkey.

## Adapting to reality

When the concept of transmedia storytelling first made headlines in academic milieu, it made its impact within the context of fictional productions (Giovagnoli, 2011; Jenkins, 2006; Scolari, 2009). Henry Jenkins' (2006) definition of the concept refers to a type of storytelling that is made more visible with the emerging convergence culture. According to Jenkins (2006), media technologies advance towards connected systems of communication, which influence the way we read, tell, and interact with stories. The contemporary participative audiences are now expecting to explore more about a story as they migrate from one medium to another. In this regard, transmedia storytelling corresponds to this mobile, interactive, and connected experience by expanding stories across diverse media channels to build an immersive storyworld. Transmedia worldbuilding in the entertainment industry is not a brand-new practice. In fact, while some sources indicate that its practice dates all the way back to Japanese media mix techniques of the 1960s (Jenkins, 2006), Freeman (2014, 2016a) goes further to say that transmedia storytelling has gone through "a far longer, far broader, and far more complex historical development" (2016a, sec. Introduction). As Jenkins clearly states in the foreword section of *The Routledge Companion to Transmedia Studies*, it was "something many of us recognised but did not yet have the words to describe" (2018, p. 3). In time, gradual changes in media production, distribution, and regulation made us even more aware of what was happening. Interconnected media systems and hypertextual communication was paving the way to a more visible transmedia structure: fictional worlds extending across media platforms.

What makes transmedia storytelling distinct from other storytelling practices is its attention to interactivity and expansion (Gambarato & Tárcia, 2017; Jenkins, 2006; Renó, 2013; Scolari, Bertetti, & Freeman, 2014). This is evident in some of the very well-known and studied transmedia worlds of the entertainment industry, such as *Star Wars* (Guynes & Hassler-Forest, 2017; Harvey, 2015; Proctor & McCulloch, 2019), *Harry Potter* (Alberti & Miller, 2018; Bell, 2019; Freeman, 2018b), and *Matrix* (Jenkins, 2006). These franchises focus on immersive experiences, where the audiences see themselves as part of the story. In order to spark exploration, these franchises also expand stories as they conquer diverse media, rather than repeating the same information over and over again. A very recent production called *SKAM*[1] is another sound example that demonstrates how deeply involved one can be to a story that makes use of transmedia storytelling principles. Ultimately, the overall goal is to construct unique story fragments that build into one big immersive storyworld. According to Jenkins (2009a, 2009b; 2010), this immersive storyworld depends upon seven core principles:

1   *Spreadability vs. drillability* (the type of engagement the consumer can have towards the story): A story can be consumed through either scanning across the media landscape in search of all of its components or drilling deeper into the context and background of the story.

2   *Continuity vs. multiplicity* (the number of perspectives the franchise is planning to have in the story): A story can be told either from a single perspective with a definitive version and ongoing coherence or from multiple perspectives with alternate versions in different contexts.

3   *Immersion vs. extractability* (what the consumer does with the story): One can either enter the world of the story or take away a part of the story into one's daily life. In this context, the story benefits from the points of blur between the real world and the fictional storyworld.

4   *Worldbuilding* (nourishes from the blur between the real world and the fictional storyworld): When a complex story is constructed with multiple storylines and perspectives dispersed across numerous media, a storyworld is built. In this storyworld, real-world and digital experiences engage, and this may lead to formation of fan communities.

5   *Seriality*: It is the possibility of telling a story in segments not through a single medium but across several media platforms.

6   *Subjectivity* (from the story's point of view): Exploring a story from new eyes of secondary characters or third parties in different contexts can provide diversity of perspective. Looking at the same events from multiple points of view can also drive the audience to consider who is speaking and who they are speaking for.

7   *Performance*: It calls for participation from the audience, "whether that may be in changing behaviour or inspiring re-enactment of the story itself" (Moloney & Unger, 2014, p. 111). It is based around whether the story lets the audience portray their own performance and contribute to the story. In order for the consumer to fully experience the fictional storyworld, Jenkins (2006) sets the following conditions:

> [...] consumers must assume the role of hunters and gatherers, chasing down bits of the story across media channels, comparing notes with each other via online discussion groups, and collaborating to ensure that everyone who invests time and effort will come away with a richer entertainment experience.
>
> (p. 21)

At a window display, looking through all the published how-to books on transmedia production (see Bernardo, 2011, 2014; Dowd, 2015; McErlean, 2018; Phillips, 2012; Pratten, 2015; Zeiser, 2015) and their manifestations in the entertainment industry (e.g. the world of Lego or Disney), the sole purpose of utilising this method looks as though just another way to build successful brands and increase market profit. However, as Carlos A. Scolari (2013; 2014) and Jenkins (2011), who are the leading scholars in the field, predicted, more comes out of these transmedia narratives than brands, entertainment, profits, and fiction. Scholars, still to this day, continue to investigate the application of transmedia storytelling approach on non-fictional or non-profit practices, such as documentary making, activism, or journalism (see Alzamora & Tárcia, 2012; Canavilhas, 2013, 2018; Gambarato, 2019; Gambarato & Tárcia, 2017; Moloney, 2011a, 2012; Renó, 2013; Veglis, 2012). The ongoing investigation yields new understandings of this concept and, just like its previously mentioned story structure, transmedia storytelling approach expands to adapt to a wide range of contexts.

It should be understandable to see why transmedia storytelling gradually finds its place within a larger scope of industries, especially after the interfluent concepts that were mentioned in Chapter 2. Although the role of transmedia storytelling in the entertainment industry, at least in the beginning, may have been an alternative method of preference, contemporary media ecology necessitates its immersive and interactive practice in any story that is told by any context. Journalism is one of these contexts, where the use of this storytelling approach is on the front burner (Gambarato & Alzamora, 2018). What

Chapter 2 pointed out is that the understanding, function, and actors of the news-making realm entered a multifaceted passage. In this passage, the search for truth lies in the interaction between the newsmakers and the public. The post-truth era motivates communities to trust sources that share their own beliefs and values, taking it hard to digest diverse opinions. Additionally, journalists are shining out more than ever for social change and dragging along the citizens, who want to participate in the news-making process. News audiences continue to be a part of change through virtual crowds. Furthermore, news organisations are renewing business models to enable and increase audience interaction within news consumption experiences. Journalists, who refuse to be a part of politically oppressed and commercialised news-making practices, are looking for business models of their own to stand up against undemocratic journalism attempts. All these dethreading instances unveil a set of characteristics for the contemporary news-making experience: *news as collective conversation, news as an immersive journey, journalist as an independent collaborator, news as personalised consumption and news making for social change.*

This interactive, immersive, collaborative, and contextual news storytelling experience is no stranger to transmedia storytelling theories and practices, especially when transmedia journalism is considered (Gambarato, 2019). Although transmedia journalism is a term that has been newly coined, the past decade has brought about a considerable amount of research, which vividly draws the outline of its theory and practice (see Alzamora & Tárcia, 2012; Freeman & Proctor, 2018; Gambarato, 2019; Gambarato & Alzamora, 2018; Gambarato & Tárcia, 2017; Moloney, 2011a; Renó, 2013). Transmedia approach in journalism is defined with diverse wording but in similar meaning by various scholars. It is an immersive news narrative that expands across multiple media platforms with the intention of audience interaction. In this immersive journey, the news consumer migrates across various online and offline news platforms "in which the audience is involved in a committed way, adding and sharing content through digital environments" (Gambarato, 2019, p. 118). It is about "creating a rich in-between space, an archive of shared meaning in-between different parts of the story" (Veglis, 2012, p. 315). What lures transmedia storytelling to journalism practice is more than contemporary means of communication technologies. By pushing immersive experience and engagement to forefront, transmedia journalism narratives build bridges of relevance and conversation between real-life news and the public (Gambarato & Tárcia, 2017; Moloney, 2011a). In other words, the public can feel a sense of deepened belonging to their surroundings. In this respect, The Sochi Project[2] (Gambarato, 2016; Hornstra & van Bruggen, 2007) and the Future of Food[3] (Godulla & Wolf, 2018; Moloney, 2015) are among many journalism projects that scholars dwell upon to understand in what ways transmedia storytelling enforces journalism practice and in which areas it needs to be reconsidered.

Journalism is a practice that claims to be committed to real-life phenomena and objective methods of verification (Kovach & Rosenstiel, 2014). Although adapting transmedia storytelling to journalism practice is possible, some aspects of its application to reality differ from fictional contexts. This specific distinction calls for a retouch of reality in the existing work on transmedia storytelling. This is where Kevin Moloney's (2011b) customised seven principles come into play. In his master's thesis on *Porting Transmedia Storytelling to Journalism*, Moloney (2011a) revisits each principle in detail from the perspective of journalism. The following brief list of revisited principles are summarised versions by Renira Rampazzo Gambarato and Lorena Peret Teixeira Tárcia (2017), who are also two of the leading scholars of this field:

> (1) spreadability (the spread of a story by users' sharing); (2) drillability (search for more details about the news; official content expansions, including social media networks); (3) continuity and seriality (maintain continuity and exploit the characteristics of each medium; keep the audience's attention for a longer period); (4) diversity (add other points of view, including those of the public); (5) immersion (generate alternative forms of storytelling for the public to delve deeper into the story); (6) extractability (apply the journalist's work in everyday life with the public commitment); (7) real world (show all shades of the news, without focusing on simplification); and (8) inspiration to action (pursue intervention by the public in real actions seeking solutions to problems).
>
> (p. 3)

Besides Moloney's perspective, various scholars revisit transmedia journalism principles to find a common set of rules that would both embrace fictional and nonfictional contexts (Canavilhas, 2013, 2018; Gambarato & Tárcia, 2017; Looney, 2013). Coming back to the debate on the relevance of transmedia storytelling in contemporary journalism practices, perhaps, Canavilhas (2013) presents the most convenient categorisation for this argument: *interactivity, hypertextuality, integrated multimodality,* and *contextualisation.* It is possible to say that these traits of transmedia journalism are familiar to some of the aspects of how we experience news today.

## Interactivity

In Canavilhas' (2013) description, interactivity occurs in various forms. It could happen in a one-way manner, just as reading a newspaper; or it could be bidirectional as reading a news article on an online website and, after finding it interesting, sharing it from a social media account. This interaction process gradually increases its effect as the users are given the option to consume only what interests them at the preferred time, such as archived podcasts or on-demand services. The highest level of interaction happens when you are given access to comment on news, add photos, or participate in forums in addition to the original content. Each of these types of interactivity also has their own high to low degrees of participation depending on their ease of interaction, the possibilities of bundling information, the cases of customisation, and the potential to control the content (Heeter, 1989). According to Canavilhas (2013), in an ideal situation for transmedia storytelling, the content must allow a high degree of interactivity that maximises all of the gradual variables listed above. However, any degree of interaction, whether it may be commenting under a news post that you have an opinion on, or redistributing a news content that interests you and that you deem important on social media, is fundamental for a narrative to be considered transmedia.

Building a certain type of relation to the news content or other users is what transmedia interaction is all about and what the contemporary news media is trying to accomplish by experimenting with the offerings of advancing media technologies. These offerings enable more than posting comments or redistributing news content. Chapter 2 dwelled upon extreme cases of interaction between journalists and citizens, who worked together in the news-making process. These cases show us a deeper sense of interaction that is happening. The passages of interaction between the content, user, and community become as clear as day when we hear the *news as a collective conversation*. Contemporary news audiences are not afraid to act (prosumers, engaged communities, and citizen journalists), and the demand for more interactive news experiences is growing day by day.

## Hypertextuality

Imagine a very large spider web of digital data. That is what the Internet offers us in a macro scale, an infinite network of data. In this network, hypertextuality represents the interconnections among digital textual information. This term has been in the literature of informatics since the 1960s (Nelson, 1965); however, in time, it was revisited in different contexts, such as literature (Mangen, 2008), journalism (Salaverría, 2005), and now transmedia storytelling (Canavilhas, 2013; Kalogeras, 2014; McErlean, 2018). As Canavilhas (2013) clarifies, hypertextuality allows you to build navigable content that can effectively inform users by using complex hypertext structures. In simple explanation, through links, you can browse around the online space to discover the information that you are interested in.

From the transmedia narrative perspective, these hypertexts and hyperlinks are crucial as they construct bridges in between stories. Specifically, in transmedia journalism, hypertextuality allows the news consumer to acknowledge a context around the given information. For instance, as you read about a mass shooting on a news website, the article includes a hyperlink to the related posts on Twitter, where you get detailed information from local witnesses. This kind of referral to outside sources provide further contextual information about the phenomenon. Furthermore, hypertextuality works as a crucial element in expanding the transmedia news story.

However, although the existing literature on hypertextuality is concentrated within the confines of the World Wide Web, this book captures the term from a broader perspective. Meaning, when an online medium (news website) directs you to an offline one (book) or when a podcast programme tells you to check out a social media account, these actions can also be viewed within the context of hypertextuality.

These connections among media are commonly constructed by content producers. As mentioned in Chapter 2, contemporary behaviours of news consumption and production portray a horizontal and nonlinear landscape. In this landscape, it is no longer the storyteller deciding on the newsworthiness and reading order of the story, but the reader drifting along the components of the story while finding ways to interact with it. Hypertextuality, in this respect, is the roadmap of this landscape, taking news consumers from one place to another to meet new characters, contexts, and storylines. The experience of *news as an immersive journey* is possible where people or events are linked to each other and news stories travel beyond medium through hyperlinks.

### Integrated multimodality

In this immersive journey, we simultaneously experience multiple semiotic sources, where we take new meanings out of each. According to Jay Lemke (2009, 2010), as we make new meanings and live our lives across the boundaries between sites and institutions, we are becoming transmedia traversals:

> Today we surf the web, jumping from screen to screen, site to site, genre to genre, source to source. And we surf a good bit of our lives, too, cycling our attention from conversation to mobile phone to advertising poster to PDA and laptop email, chat, and video. These random or creative traversals as I have begun to call them (Lemke, 2005a) appear symptomatic not just of viewing habits, but of lives. The defining characteristic of a traversal is that it makes meaning across boundaries: between media, genres, sites, institutions, contexts.
>
> (2010, p. 579)

In this perspective, transmedia narratives reinforce this wandering behaviour with its structural promise of multimodality. Transmedia multimodality refers to the "interplay between discrete semiotic modes that occur across, and within, different media when they are positioned as parts of a singular narrative ecology" (Lynch, McGowan, & Hancox, 2017, para. 5). Traversals are invited to make meaning out of media-specific representations of storyworlds that exist in narrative cohesion (Lynch et al., 2017). In a simple wording, transmedia multimodality entails the use of various forms of media while constructing an integrated storyworld. Each medium offers different views of meaning-making, ways of representation, and different paths of interaction to its content (Dena, 2010; Jenkins, 2011). According to Canavilhas (2013), in the context of transmedia journalism, deciding on when to use image in a social media post, sound in a news podcast, or text in a news article holds a specific purpose and needs to be integrated in the overall context of the transmedia news story. This purpose could be simply to confirm information, highlighting something, or illustrate a particular situation for clarification (Canavilhas, 2013). In an additional perspective, multimodality offers a way to extend a news narrative through unique affordances of distinct media choices.

In contexts where getting reliable news or any kind of news is hard, representation of truth in the most objective and accessible way becomes crucial. Each medium that is used in the meaning-making process has utmost importance for the information that is communicated. Independent journalism practices are now a vital part of integrated multimodality, as they guide traversals from one news media source to another. Transmedia traversals of Lemke (2010), in this respect, take the form of the aforementioned micro audiences of Batsell (2015). People, in search of reliable news sources, gather around organisations or individuals, who they can trust. In quest of delivering the most suitable representation of truth, perhaps, a *journalist's role as an independent moderator* enables an expansive and interconnected experience through multimodal news sources. However, how these independent news sources make use of multiple media forms and channels is still an area that needs to be covered. The cases in Chapter 4 dwell upon the aspect of multimodality in independent transmedia journalism narratives.

## Contextualisation

The last one of transmedia journalism traits minds the context of consumption space of the user. According to Canavilhas (2013), the increasing mobility of audiences, the miniaturisation and diversification of platforms with constant internet connection, the individual consumption of the contents and the avalanche of information received daily are variables that potentiate transmedia journalism. However, these aspects also condition the way transmedia journalism is practised, requiring levels of contextualisation adapted to users' consumption habits. Dragging the consumer's attention to content and giving the content visibility in the eyes of the consumer requires a degree of content personalisation (Canavilhas, 2013). This is possible through "understanding of the narrative within the migratory behaviour of the public" (Bicalho, 2019, p. 206).

In the course of a day, a traversal lives through various media practices, visiting various representational spaces and flows. Among the overlapping fragments of a news story that is told from multiple media sources, each individual consumes the story in different compositions, from distinct consumption patterns (Bicalho, 2019). However, the busy and complex environment makes it even more difficult to spark curiosity and interest through any content. Transmedia journalism aims to encourage public participation by building variations of time and space in the overall storyworld. It aims to adapt to the consumer's daily routine by offering new entrances and interaction paths to the news story, turning *news into a personalised consumption experience*.

## Diving deeper and deeper

Up until now, we have witnessed various characteristic similarities between transmedia storytelling and contemporary journalism practices.

Scolari (2013a) has foreseen this similarity as he describes the inevitable relation between the transformation of journalism and development of transmedia studies. This perspective also opens up a research area where today's complex journalism practices can be read through theories and practices of transmediality, which is what *Exploring Transmedia Journalism in The Digital Age* (2018) mainly touches upon. However, this book's perspective towards transmediality does not only consist of its technological elements or structural principles. Recent studies on transmediality emphasise on its ontological function to "shape—and to re-shape—how we perceive the media and the world around it" (Freeman & Gambarato, 2018b, p. 18). At this deeper level, theoretical borders of transmediality expand to diverse contexts of cultural perspectives, such as heritage, politics, education, and religion (Freeman & Gambarato, 2018b; Freeman & Proctor, 2018). These studies on cultures of transmediality position humans at the centre and work around issues of media and communication to better understand and improve the transmedia experience. As Freeman and Gambarato (2018a) indicate, transmedia cultures are "experience-centred, technologically augmented conversations, a sharing between storytellers and audiences, between audiences and other audiences, and between online and offline worlds" (p. 21).

A common element that one of these cultures of transmediality shares with journalism is, perhaps, the element of social change. It is no mystery that people hold the power to transform cultural and social institutions through their interactions and relationships. The long list of social movements in our history promotes this statement: The Suffragettes' long fight for women's right to vote in America; the global #MeToo movement against sexual harassment and sexual assault; or LGBT social movements that stand up for the people of LGBT in society. In order to use their powers for positive social change, people need to understand what is at stake, find ways of interaction to address shared concerns, and move collectively for a solution (Downman & Ubayasiri, 2017). Both journalism and transmedia practices play parts in this scenario. On the one hand, journalism is still one of the most important influencers of social movements, aiming to keep the society aware of its surroundings whenever and however, and impelling people to action if necessary (Downman & Ubayasiri, 2017). On the other hand, immersive and inclusive nature of transmedia narratives embraces society's heightened sense of engagement to their surroundings (Freeman, 2018c). Large communities form around narratives ready to support the cause and act for change.

## Transmedia journalism and social change

When asked for The Refugee Journalism Project[4] to share her thoughts on journalists' influence on social change, Nargess Tavassolian, an Iranian journalist and legal analyst, replied: "I believe journalism is the single most powerful tool for social change, that is worth every risk and all the hard work required" (Cropper, 2016, para. 28). Coming from a country where there are many taboo subjects that are not publicly talked about, Tavassolian cannot ignore the utmost significance journalism has on giving voice to the voiceless, and push the society forward to break these taboos. This responsibility of acting as agents of social change in politics, economy, culture, and everyday life puts on a very heavy weight on journalists. In their book, titled *Journalism for Social Change in Asia*, Scott Downman and Kasun Ubayasiri clearly describe these weights. In fact, it would be next to impossible to put it into better words; therefore, I prefer to share the following long section as follows:

> Firstly, change cannot be enacted unless problems or issues are identified. An important aspect of journalism for social change is that it must identify something that needs to be changed. Whether that is an issue, a problem, an injustice or an abuse, there is a clear need to shine a light on something hidden or not clearly understood. Secondly, journalism for social change is a service designed to alert, inform and educate society. This idea of journalism as a service, rather than just viewing it as a profession or career, gives journalism a clear sense of purpose. Journalism for social change does not just view journalism as reporting but a process through which the presentation of varied viewpoints, ideas and opinions gives society the capacity to make informed decisions about the future. Thirdly, rather than falling into the trap of advertising, journalism for social change does not sell something, it gives society something. This distinction is important, because rather than serving as a platform for entertainment, journalism for social change is often invested in giving society the information tools and mechanisms necessary for making change. Lastly, journalism for social change is about either finding, or at least proposing solutions.
>
> (2017, Chapter Preface)

However, what Downman and Ubayasiri described in these lines is the ideal picture of what it should be rather than what it actually is in the real world. Journalists all around the world face political, economic, or social barriers that they have to push through, or sometimes maybe give in. Firstly, in countries where press freedom is threatened by ruling governments, journalists struggle to find effective communication outlets to reach the public. Secondly, in contemporary digital media culture where the news industry faces economic uncertainties, the journalists are forced to comply to commercial constraints. Lastly, in some cases, journalists face social pressures where the society is reluctant to change. Saba Bebawi, in her book on *Investigative Journalism in the Arab World* (2016), describes the issues and challenges journalists face in social environments where it is believed that uncovering the truth and being critical of social, religious, and cultural taboos destroy a country.

Another side to this dark picture presents how we actually need journalists now, more than ever. As political, economic, or social realms shift towards harmful ends for society, accurate awareness of our surroundings becomes the "iron core" of democratic public discourse (Hirst, 2011). As mentioned previously, the power to change what is wrong is in the hands of the people. However, positive change is only possible through careful collection, analysis, interpretation, definition, and reporting of accurate information. A society that gives in to news censorship, commercialisation, or taboos, therefore, faces the risk of being a dysfunctional society that is waiting to rupture.

Having the responsibility of informing the public about the truth, journalists, as narrators, also have to use effective ways to evoke the public's desire to act and make the extra effort to support communities outside of their own. Grabbing the public's attention through the clutter of information is not an easy task. Especially in the age of constant access to excessive data flowing in from countless sources. However, along its disadvantages, the contemporary media technologies also offer us an advantage of having the means to form a globally networked society ready to act when necessary (Rainie & Wellman, 2012). What is left for the journalists to discover is ways of conveying news to the public through "effective narrative representations of complex issues and immersive experiences for audiences" (Hancox, 2018, p. 467).

Transmedia storytelling, in this context, becomes a purposive approach in grabbing the attention of the public by placing the power of the narrative at the forefront, using ubiquitous media outlets, decentralising the concept of authorship, and engaging users through participation (Hancox, 2018; Lovato, 2018; Weinreich, 2011). Firstly, telling stories of real-life phenomena has always been what journalism is all about. Through journalistic narratives, we learn about the reality that surrounds us and give meaning to our experiences. These investigative stories play an important role in social change, as change happens within individuals and communities, who are empowered by telling their own stories (Hancox, 2018). Advances in media technologies also have significant influence on the effectiveness of these narratives. Reaching more people from a deeper level through interactive and collaborative technologies is what journalists are still experimenting on (Lovato, 2018). On that note, transmedia storytelling proposes journalists to forget about the former norms of linear narrative structure and plot and guides them to produce a network of stories customised for specific audiences or media channels (Hancox, 2018). The power of the narrative, in this case, applies in reaching the public on a more emotional level through personalised ways of communication. Secondly, grabbing the attention of the public is possible through encompassing them with information blooming from numerous channels of communication. This is one of the reasons why using multiple media channels is key in transmedia storytelling. As mentioned in the section about *contextualisation*, this all-round narrative structure can offer content to audiences in forms or channels that are convenient to their everyday routine. By doing so, the story can infuse into one's daily life seamlessly. Thirdly, social change, as we mentioned, is a work of many. While it captures the unheard voices and unseen communities in a society, it takes heart from diverse opinions of diverse individuals. In this sense, transmedia narrative structure that embraces the decentralised concept of authorship can provide multiple platforms for many voices to be heard, where many perspectives of a story are cherished (Hancox, 2018). Lastly, and perhaps most importantly, social change calls the public to act towards things that needs changing. Nothing can stay constant. Time makes sure of that. A system that may have been working for a society fifty years ago could be crumbling today due to various contextual changes that occurred, such as technology, economy, nature, or migrations. When the system loses its grip on a society, people of that society expect change. In order to get it, they need to act and engage with the communities that share the same need for change. Participation and performance are also major aspects of transmedia narratives. The idea behind this perspective is to encourage the audience to participate in the storyworld through various paths of engagement. As the audience participates within the story, the more connected they feel to what is being told, share their own story and, perhaps, feel a sense of belonging.

These connection points make transmedia narratives all the more useful for journalists to encourage the public on their pursuit of social change. An example, at this point, may provide clarity in what I mean. In 2016, Ken Armstrong and T. Christian Miller won a Pulitzer Prize for their reporting project, *An Unbelievable Story of Rape* (Miller & Armstrong, 2015). The story became such a hit that it resumed its popularity on Netflix in 2019 as a miniseries, *Unbelievable*. However, few people realise that this story is actually just the tip of an iceberg. *An Unbelievable Story of Rape* was, in fact, a part of a series of news articles and a collaboration effort between The Marshall Project and ProPublica, both of which are non-profit newsrooms that focus on investigative journalism. This example centres upon The Marshall Project, due to its more apparent transmedia structure. The project, which was founded in 2014, "seeks to create and sustain a sense of national urgency about the U.S. criminal justice system" (The Marshall Project, 2014a). It covers diverse topics regarding issues of prison population, death penalty, immigration, juvenile justice, mental health, policing, politics and reform, and race. Parallel to these topics of enquiry, the project also hosts ongoing specific projects on limited events or contexts, such as personal stories of people who work or live in the criminal justice system (Life Inside) and the state of executions in different parts of the United States presented in infographics and timelines (The Next to Die). The project team consists of people from diverse areas of news and digital industry, such as investigative journalists, digital content producers, news editors, and veteran crime reporters (The Marshall Project, 2014b). The project website (themarshallproject.org) is not the only platform that is used to reach audiences. The team shares their reporting on variety of other partnering news channels, such as *The New York Times*, *The Washington Post*, and *The Texas Tribune*. Aiming to educate and enlarge audiences on diverse issues of American criminal justice system, the projects use social media platforms (Facebook, Twitter and YouTube) to share their news articles, reports, first-person essays, and stories that are told by relatives of the convicted. The project is also open to participation through social media accounts and personal letters of experiences relating to the subject. This example, in general, demonstrates how transmedia narratives can be utilised by journalists to communicate a complex issue in its multi-layered form. How much do we know about what goes on behind bars? How far does the civil rights of people reach in the criminal justice system? The Marshall Project delivers diverse perspectives and personal stories to convey understanding and empathy for the lesser known life inside American prisons. Revealing the unknown to the public is where social change begins its journey. By using powerful narrative strategies, ubiquitous media outlets, numerous partnering authors, and audience engagement, this journalism project demonstrates a proper example of how transmedia storytelling can be an effective method in constituting change.

### Transmedia ethos

If we dive deeper into the role of transmedia spaces in uniting people for a cause, we may find another layer of connection. This implicit layer, transmedia ethos, is described in the latest studies of scholars as an additional lens to read transmedia ecosystem from a cultural perspective (Freeman, 2016b, 2018a, 2018c; Freeman & Taylor-Ashfield, 2017). What transmedia ethos indicates is that rather than only following stories told across media, audiences follow common meanings, values, beliefs, needs, themes, and philosophies. They are encouraged to visit and engage with content that has similar underlying beliefs and values (Freeman, 2016b). The word *ethos* in this combination is not read as tangible characters, stories or brands, "but rather as a much more fluid, ephemeral and value-laden" level of attachment (Freeman & Gambarato, 2018a, p. 22). In such an abstract connection, fragments of the storyworld can "derive from completely different broadcaster and producer contexts" (Freeman, 2018c, p. 434).

Matthew Freeman, a leading scholar on this perspective, goes even further and bases the position of transmedia ethos within the boundaries of cultural alternativism (Freeman, 2018a). What Freeman suggests is "an emphatic sense of alternativism to mainstream media cultures" (Freeman, 2018a, para. 18). In other words, transmedia ethos helps to form alternative cultures when mainstream media falls short of representation due to political consequences, legal barriers, or moral values of a given society. A proper example to this situation can be observed regarding the representation of LGBT culture. Firstly, authoritarian regimes, such as the regime of Russia, impose political consequences to pro-LGBT content (Persson, 2014). By classifying homosexual content as an act of propaganda, the Russian regime reflects a sense of fear in mainstream media institutions and prevent the visibility of LGBT culture to masses. Secondly, there are countries, such as Egypt or Malaysia, that criminalise homosexuality (Human Dignity Trust, 2014). In countries such as Libya and Algeria, maximum punishment for homosexual behaviour is imprisonment and paying a fine. Moreover, in countries such as Tanzania, Sudan, and Nigeria, this punishment, respectively, evolves into life in prison, death penalty, and even death by stoning. In these mentioned countries, the serious life and death consequence of homosexual behaviour eliminates any kind of visibility of its culture in the mainstream realm. Thirdly, there are societies, such as the Turkish society, who find it hard to integrate homosexuality to their moral fabric (Hürriyet Daily News, 2019; Karakaş, 2019). Moral pressures of society have the power to cost you your job, your friends, and your family. In such a context, it would be naive to expect the visibility of LGBT culture in the mainstream layer. All the factors above, and many more that has not been mentioned, prevent the LGBT community to find a place among mainstream media cultures. However, outside of the mainstream, shared beliefs and values, together with the means of alternative media, enable this culture to find a place, visibility, in some part of society, rather than tucking it away like it does not exist. Transmedia ethos, nourished by these common values, beliefs, and needs, is formed within a participatory communication network through different media channels. In these spaces of communication, the LGBT community, or other cultures that share the same fate of invisibility, can manifest and flourish by reaching a global audience.

But how does transmedia ethos form such a strong bond? Two major points of influence come to the fore: *heightened sense of engagement* and *organic formation of a community*. Although Freeman (2018c) explains his reasoning behind this bond from the context of a charity campaign (the BBC's Red Nose Day), I believe the same approach can be applied to any type of vision that hopes to gather and mobilise a society for positive change. Coming back to a prior example, The Marshall Project, gathers stories from prisoners, relatives of prisoners, employees of the American criminal justice system, and other actors, who are related to the case. All of these stories, flowing from various media channels, aim to attract people who care about criminal justice reform (The Marshall Project, 2014a). Aside from the story itself, the project also aims to capture people who value nonpartisan and non-profit investigative journalism. Through interactive paths and emphatic content, the project encourages people, who share the same belief, to emotionally engage with the story and feel a sense of deepened belonging. The heightened sense of engagement through transmedia ethos, in return, provides a system of support from the audience. In the case of The Marshall Project, we can see an online community forming organically around its social media platforms. A closed discussion group is also dedicated to the project, which has 832 members sharing thoughts on news and conversations about the death penalty in America (The Marshall Project, 2018). This Facebook group is only one tangible example of the emotional support the project receives. Out of almost 80.000 followers, both on Facebook and

Twitter, perhaps, this community expands even further with people who participate through different degrees of engagement. Moreover, the support system does not only involve the emotional but also the financial aspects of the project. The members of the community, who feel as a part of the story and want to sustain its impact, do not hesitate to contribute financially to the cause. On that note, The Marshall Project receives a sustainable stream of revenue from funders, such as non-profit foundations, organisations, and individuals (The Marshall Project, 2014c).

## Transmedia survival

Up until now, we addressed transmediality in journalism from its characteristic properties to its value-laden perspective (transmedia ethos). If we were to remember the title of this chapter, trace our steps all the way back to the beginning and ask the same question again: How does the notion of transmediality, among other efforts, serve as a golden string to rethread what is ripped apart from the fabric of journalism in Turkey? It is clear to see that this question lays on top of a fabric that covers a complex web of meanings, rituals, conventions, and symbol systems, in other words, a complex fabric of culture (Zelizer, 2005, 2017). In this regard, transmediality can be questioned as a way of life, finding its place within the cultural fabric of independent journalism in Turkey (Freeman & Proctor, 2018, p. 32). This specific context gives us an opportunity to explore a new manifestation of transmediality that rises among new formations of journalism: transmediality as a framework of survival.

For the sake of rethreading the broken pieces of journalism in Turkey, perhaps, acknowledging all the broken parts along with the missing ones and their variations is the most reasonable way to follow. What I mean by that is the inclusion of every perspective of journalism, as a profession, industry, institution, or as a craft (Zelizer, 2005, 2017). The interfluent state of definitions, behaviours, and governance of journalism all around the world makes it all the more necessary to approach this issue from a cultural perspective. Different approaches to journalism are not only observed on a global scale but also, on a micro level, among the independent news initiatives in Turkey. Regarding journalism as a culture, for this investigation, is key to understanding the dynamic conventions, routines, and practices of independent journalism initiatives in Turkey within their history and context (Zelizer, 2005, 2017).

Focusing on Turkey, we face media ownership concentration and political polarisation along with judicial injustice which makes it harder for journalists to maintain their ethical stance. Independent journalism initiatives, as they fight for a democratic society, struggle to survive financially, structurally, ethically, and legally. Many factors (historical, social, economic, political, moral, ideological, and technological) can be listed as to what shaped the culture of independent journalism in Turkey to what it is now. Not all, but some of these factors were mentioned in Chapter 2. It is a culture that is trying to survive on many levels within a complex habitat. Within this habitat, these independent journalism initiatives shape into new forms. What this investigation intends to see is how much of a role transmediality plays in these new cultural formations (Freeman & Proctor, 2018).

Let's also not forget a journalist's role within the fabric of a news culture. After all, journalists perform a major part as they "impart preference statements about what is good and bad, moral and amoral and appropriate and inappropriate in the world" (Zelizer, 2004, p. 177). In other words, they are the conductors, who shape the news, therefore, influence the ideas and actions of their audiences as well. In the case of Turkey, news culture cannot be considered independent of Turkish society and the political climate. There is a constant circular interaction as the society, journalism, and politics influence one another. At first, the political climate is reflected in journalism culture and shapes it accordingly. Journalism culture, in return, shapes the public opinion through its doings. Therefore, the interaction has a structure that feeds each other, placing journalists within an important position of power.

This research perceives the independent journalism initiatives' call for social change as an embracing of a cultural stance. Their efforts come together to impel positive social change through the power of prioritising diversity of opinion and balanced arguments all in the common cause of freedom of expression and building a democratic society. Can we observe these efforts from the fresh perspective of transmediality? At the beginning of this chapter, we have observed similarities between recent global journalism culture and transmediality. In the context of journalism in Turkey, the efforts to maintain moral responsibility and positional integrity have led journalists to independent approaches that embed new frameworks of survival within Turkish journalism culture. Transmediality is, perhaps, one of these frameworks of support, as this chapter presents it as a methodological map to this research. In order to demonstrate this framework, Chapter 4 investigates the role transmediality plays within the new independent journalism formations in Turkey. Reading these formations through the lens of transmediality opens up a fresh perspective into its role in journalism, not only as an immersive story experience but also as a way of life. Moreover, this context also offers us to question whether transmedia journalism is gradually shifting from being only a commercial entity to becoming a political system for social change.

## Notes

1 *SKAM* first launched as a Norwegian teen drama web series that told the story of a couple of teenagers' daily lives. The web series told the story through short videos that were posted online in real-time moments, WhatsApp messages sent among the characters, and social media posts shared from accounts of fictional characters. Norwegian audience was able to follow the story of each character together or separately by following their social media accounts, subscribing to *SKAM* story updates, and interacting with the characters through own posts, comments. The web series became such a success that it broke streaming records of a Norwegian Broadcasting Corporation channel. *SKAM*'s success led to its adaptation in numerous countries, such as France, Belgium, Germany, Italy, the United States, Spain, and the Netherlands. In 2018, the web series' showrunner Julie Andem also published *SKAM* books, which featured some of the original manuscripts of the story that were never filmed.

2 In the years between 2007 and 2014, a Dutch documentary photographer Rob Hornstra and journalist/filmmaker Arnold van Bruggen told a non-fiction narrative about the hidden story behind the 2014 Winter Olympic Games in Sochi, Russia (Hornstra & van Bruggen, 2007). The story revealed the changes that occurred in the city of Sochi, from the beginning of the preparations up until the event ended, and diverse stories that conflict with the positive picture portrayed by the Russian mainstream news media (Gambarato, 2016). The project consisted of an interactive documentary website, print materials such as books, cards and newspapers, e-books, social media platforms, and gallery exhibitions.

3 In 2014, National Geographic launched The Future of Food as an eight-month series transmedia journalism project to investigate how to meet the growing need for nourishment without harming the planet. Unlike most organisations, when National Geographic Society launched the Future of Food Project, its media structure held within various content creation and distribution platforms such as magazines, books, TV channels, and even a museum. The editors and managers from Society's various media platforms gathered to collaborate on a transmedia journalism experience (Godulla & Wolf, 2018; Moloney, 2015). Journalists within and outside of the organisation generated lots of content on the growing need for nourishment to be distributed in the form of text, photos, or video. During the eight months of the project, the audience was informed with posts on social media, articles in magazines, recipe sessions in galleries, and lectures from experts (Moloney, 2015).

4 The Refugee Journalism Project was launched in 2016 aiming to assist refugee and exiled journalists to resume their profession in the United Kingdom. With the partnership of Migrant Resource Centre, since 2018, the project is based at the London College of Communication, part of the University of the Arts London (Refugee Journalism Project, 2018).

# References

Alberti, J., & Miller, P. A. (Eds.). (2018). *Transforming Harry: The Adaptation of Harry Potter in the Transmedia Age*. Wayne State University Press.

Alzamora, G., & Tárcia, L. (2012). Convergence and transmedia: Semantic galaxies and emergent narratives in journalism. *Brazilian Journalism Research*. Retrieved from http://bjr.sbpjor.org.br/bjr/article/view/407

Batsell, J. (2015). *Engaged Journalism: Connecting with Digitally Empowered News Audiences*. Columbia University Press.

Bebawi, S. (2016). *Investigative Journalism in the Arab World*. Palgrave Macmillan.

Bell, C. E. (2019). *Transmedia Harry Potter: Essays on Storytelling across Platforms*. McFarland, Incorporated, Publishers.

Bernardo, N. (2011). *The Producer's Guide to Transmedia: How to Develop, Fund, Produce and Distribute Compelling Stories Across Multiple Platforms*. Beactive Books.

Bernardo, N. (2014). *Transmedia 2.0: How to Create an Entertainment Brand using a Transmedial Approach to Storytelling*. Beactive Books.

Bicalho, L. A. G. (2019). Potential Mediations of Hashtags within Transmedia Journalism. *Journalism and Ethics*, 743–762. doi:10.4018/978-1-5225-8359-2.ch040

Canavilhas, J. (2013). Jornalismo Transmídia: Um Desafio ao Velho Ecossistema Midiático. In D. Renó, C. Campalans, S. Ruiz, & V. Gosciola (Eds.), *Periodismo Transmedia: Miradas múltiples* (pp. 53–68). Editorial Universidad del Rosario.

Canavilhas, J. (2018). Journalism in the twenty-first century: To be or not to be transmedia? In R. R. Gambarato & G. C. Alzamora (Eds.), *Exploring Transmedia Journalism in the Digital Age* (pp. 1–14). IGI Global.

Cropper, J. (2016, June 28). Journalism as a tool for truth and social change. Retrieved September 29, 2019, from The Refugee Journalism Project website: http://migrantjournalism.org/2016/06/28/journalism-as-a-tool-for-truth-and-social-change-nargess-tavassolian-expresses-her-view-on-journalism-through-her-personal-experience/

Dena, C. (2010). *Transmedia practice: Theorising the practice of expressing a fictional world across distinct media and environments* (Phd; G. Goggin, Ed.). University of Sydney.

Dowd, T. (2015). *Storytelling Across Worlds: Transmedia for Creatives and Producers*. CRC Press.

Downman, S., & Ubayasiri, K. (2017). *Journalism for Social Change in Asia: Reporting Human Rights*. Springer.

Freeman, M. (2014). Advertising the yellow brick road: Historicizing the industrial emergence of transmedia storytelling. *International Journal of Communication Systems*, 8(0), 19.

Freeman, M. (2016a). *Historicising Transmedia Storytelling: Early Twentieth-Century Transmedia Story Worlds*. Routledge.

Freeman, M. (2016b). Small change – Big difference: Tracking the transmediality of red nose day. *View: Journal of European Television History and Culture*, 5(10), 87–96.

Freeman, M. (2018a). New paths in transmediality as vast narratives. In P. Brembilla & I. A. De Pascalis (Eds.), *Reading Contemporary Serial Television Universes: A Narrative Ecosystem Framework* (pp. 9–26). Routledge.

Freeman, M. (2018b). Transmedia attractions: The case of Warner Bros. Studio tour—the Making of Harry Potter. In M. Freeman & R. R. Gambarato (Eds.), *The Routledge Companion to Transmedia Studies* (pp. 124–130). Routledge.

Freeman, M. (2018c). Transmedia charity: Constructing the ethos of the BBC's red nose day across media. In M. Freeman & R. R. Gambarato (Eds.), *The Routledge Companion to Transmedia Studies* (pp. 306–313). Routledge.

Freeman, M., & Gambarato, R. R. (2018a). Introduction: Transmedia studies—Where now? In M. Freeman & R. R. Gambarato (Eds.), *The Routledge Companion to Transmedia Studies* (pp. 1–12). Routledge.

Freeman, M., & Gambarato, R. R. (2018b). *The Routledge Companion to Transmedia Studies*. Routledge. doi:10.4324/9781351054904

Freeman, M., & Proctor, W. (2018). *Global Convergence Cultures: Transmedia Earth*. Routledge.

Freeman, M., & Taylor-Ashfield, C. (2017). "I read comics from a feminis-tic point of view": Conceptualizing the transmedia ethos of the Captain Marvel fan community. *The Journal of Fandom Studies, 5*, 317–335. doi:10.1386/jfs.5.3.317_1

Gambarato, R. R. (2016). The Sochi project: Slow journalism within the transmedia space. *Digital Journalism, 4*(4), 445–461.

Gambarato, R. R. (2019). Transmedia Journalism: The potentialities of trans-media dynamics in the news coverage of planned events. In M. Freeman & R. R. Gambarato (Eds.), *The Routledge Companion to Transmedia Studies* (pp. 118–124). Routledge.

Gambarato, R. R., & Alzamora, G. C. (2018). *Exploring Transmedia Journalism in the Digital Age*. IGI Global.

Gambarato, R. R., & Tárcia, L. P. T. (2017). Transmedia Strategies in Journal-ism: An analytical model for the news coverage of planned events. *Journalism Studies, 18*(11), 1381–1399.

Giovagnoli, M. (2011). *Transmedia Storytelling: Imagery, Shapes and Techniques*. ETC Press.

Godulla, A., & Wolf, C. (2018). Future of food: Transmedia strategies of na-tional geographic. In R. R. Gambarato & G. C. Alzamora (Eds.), *Exploring Transmedia Journalism in the Digital Age* (pp. 162–182). IGI Global.

Guynes, S., & Hassler-Forest, D. Eds. (2017). *Star Wars and the History of Transmedia Storytelling* Amsterdam University Press.

Hancox, D. (2018). Transmedia for social change. *The Routledge Companion to Transmedia Studies*, pp. 332–339. doi:10.4324/9781351054904-37

Harvey, C. B. (2015). Material myths and nostalgia-play in Star Wars. In C. B. Harvey (Ed.), *Fantastic Transmedia: Narrative, Play and Memory Across Science Fiction and Fantasy Storyworlds* (pp. 137–162). Palgrave Macmillan UK.

Heeter, C. (1989). Implications of new interactive technologies for conceptualizing communication. In J. L. Salvaggio & J. Bryant (Eds.), *Media Use in the Information Age: Emerging Patterns of Adoption and Consumer Use* (pp. 217–235). Routledge.

Hirst, M. (2011). *News 2.0: Can Journalism Survive the Internet?* Allen & Unwin Sydney.

Hornstra, R., & van Bruggen, A. (2007). About. Retrieved August 21, 2019, from The Sochi Project website: www.thesochiproject.org/en/about/

Human Dignity Trust. (2014). Map of countries that criminalise LGBT people. Retrieved October 5, 2019, from Human Dignity Trust website: https://www.humandignitytrust.org/lgbt-the-law/map-of-criminalisation/

Hürriyet Daily News. (2019, May 15). Turkey 2nd most restrictive country on gay rights in Europe – Turkey News. Retrieved October 6, 2019, from Hürriyet Daily News website: www.hurriyetdailynews.com/turkey-2nd-most-restrictive-country-on-gay-rights-in-europe-143439

Jenkins, H. (2006). *Convergence Culture: Where Old and New Media Collide.* NYU Press.

Jenkins, H. (2009a). Revenge of the origami unicorn: The remaining four principles of transmedia storytelling. Retrieved August 27, 2019, from Confessions of an Aca-Fan website: http://henryjenkins.org/blog/2009/12/revenge_of_the_origami_unicorn.html

Jenkins, H. (2009b). The revenge of the origami unicorn: seven principles of transmedia storytelling (Well, Two Actually. Five More on Friday). Retrieved August 27, 2019, from Confessions of an Aca-Fan website: http://henryjenkins.org/2009/12/the_revenge_of_the_origami_uni.html

Jenkins, H. (2010). Transmedia education: The 7 principles revisited. *Confessions of an Aca-Fan.* Retrieved from http://henryjenkins.org/blog/2010/06/transmedia_education_the_7_pri.html

Jenkins, H. (2011, August 1). Transmedia 202: Further reflections. Retrieved May 4, 2017, from Confessions of an Aca-Fan website: http://henryjenkins.org/2011/08/defining_transmedia_further_re.html

Jenkins, H. (2018). Foreword. In M. Freeman & R. R. Gambarato (Eds.), *The Routledge Companion to Transmedia Studies* (pp. 1–7). Routledge.

Kalogeras, S. (2014). *Transmedia Storytelling and the New Era of Media Convergence in Higher Education:* Palgrave Macmillan UK.

Karakaş, B. (2019, March 17). Turkey: Being gay could cost you your job. Retrieved October 6, 2019, from Deutsche Welle website: www.dw.com/en/turkey-being-gay-could-cost-you-your-job/a-47948085

Kovach, B., & Rosenstiel, T. (2014). *The Elements of Journalism: What Newspeople Should Know and the Public Should Expect.* Three Rivers Press.

Lemke, J. (2009). Multimodal genres and transmedia traversals: Social semiotics and the political economy of the sign. *Semiotica, 2009*(173), 173.

Lemke, J. (2010). Transmedia traversals: Marketing meaning and identity. *Interdisciplinary Perspectives on Multimodality: Theory and Practice.* Proceedings of the Third International Conference on Multimodality. Palladino.

Looney, M. (2013, January 30). 5 tips for transmedia storytelling. Retrieved August 31, 2019, from Mediashift website: http://mediashift.org/2013/01/5-tips-for-transmedia-storytelling030/

Lovato, A. (2018). The transmedia script for nonfictional narratives. In R. R. Gambarato & G. C. Alzamora (Eds.), *Exploring transmedia journalism in the digital age* (pp. 235–252). IGI Global.

Lynch, D., McGowan, L., & Hancox, D. (2017). Iterative multimodality: An exploration of approaches to transmedia writing. *TEXT: Journal of Writing and Writing Courses, 21*(2). Retrieved from http://eprints.qut.edu.au/114299

Mangen, A. (2008). Hypertext fiction reading: Haptics and immersion. *Journal of Research in Reading, 31*(4), 404–419.

McErlean, K. (2018). *Interactive Narratives and Transmedia Storytelling: Creating Immersive Stories across New Media Platforms.* Routledge.

Miller, T. C., & Armstrong, K. (2015). An unbelievable story of rape. Retrieved 2019, from The Marshall Project website: www.themarshallproject.org/2015/12/16/an-unbelievable-story-of-rape

Moloney, K. (2011a). *Porting transmedia storytelling to journalism* (Master of Arts, University of Denver; A. Russell, Ed.). Retrieved from http://bit.ly/2DDTa03

Moloney, K. (2011b). Transmedia journalism in principle. Retrieved February 2018, from Transmedia Journalism: Porting Transmedia Journalism to the News Business website: https://transmediajournalism.org/2011/11/23/transmedia-journalism-in-principle/

Moloney, K. (2012). *Transmedia Journalism as a Post-Digital Narrative* (No. ATLAS TR 2012-11-02). Retrieved from University of Colorado Boulder's ATLAS Institute website: www.colorado.edu/journalism/photojournalism/Transmedia_Journalism_as_a_Post-Digtal_Narrative.pdf

Moloney, K. (2015). *Future of story: Transmedia journalism and National Geographic's Future of Food project* (Doctor of Philosophy, University of Colorado; M. Winokur, Ed.). Retrieved from http://scholar.colorado.edu/atlas_gradetds/6

Moloney, K., & Unger, M. (2014). Transmedia Storytelling in Science Communication: One Subject, Multiple Media, Unlimited Stories. In J. L. Drake, Y. Y. Kontar and S. G. Rife (Eds.), *Advances in Natural and Technological Hazards Research. New Trends in Earth-Science Outreach and Engagement* (pp. 109–120). Springer

Nelson, T. (1965). A file structure for the complex. In *The Changing and the Indeterminate, ACM 20th National Conference.*

Persson, E. (2014). Banning "homosexual propaganda": Belonging and visibility in contemporary Russian media. *Sexuality & Culture, 19*(2), 256–274.

Phillips, A. (2012). *A Creator's Guide to Transmedia Storytelling: How to Captivate and Engage Audiences Across Multiple Platforms.* McGraw-Hill Education.

Pratten, R. (2015). *Getting Started in Transmedia Storytelling: A Practical Guide for Beginners* (2nd Edition). CreateSpace Independent Publishing Platform.

Proctor, W., & McCulloch, R. (2019). *Disney's Star Wars: Forces of Production, Promotion, and Reception.* University of Iowa Press.

Rainie, L., & Wellman, B. (2012). *Networked: The New Social Operating System.* MIT Press.

Refugee Journalism Project. (2018). About Us. Retrieved October 1, 2019, from The Refugee Journalism Project website: http://migrantjournalism. org/about-us-2/

Renó, D. (2013). Transmedia journalism and the new media ecology: Possible languages. In D. Renó, C. Campalans, S. Ruiz and V. Gosciola (Eds.), *Periodismo Transmedia: Miradas Múltiples* (pp. 3–19). Editorial Universidad del Rosario.

Salaverría, R. (2005). *Redacción periodística en Internet.* Eunsa.

Scolari, C. A. (2009). Transmedia storytelling: Implicit consumers, narrative worlds, and branding in contemporary media production. *International Journal of Communication, 3,* 586–606.

Scolari, C. A. (2013a). Lostology: Transmedia storytelling and expansion/ compression strategies. *Semiotica.* Retrieved from https://www.degruyter. com/view/j/semi.2013.2013.issue-195/sem-2013-0038/sem-2013-0038.xml

Scolari, C. A. (2013b). *Narrativas Transmedia: Cuando Todos Los Medios Cuentan.* Grupo Planeta (GBS).

Scolari, C. A. (2014). Transmedia storytelling: New ways of communicating in the digital age. In J. Celaya (Ed.), *Anuario ACIE de Cultura Digital: Focus 2014: The Use of New Technologies in the Performing Arts* (pp. 68–79). Acción Cultural Española.

Scolari, C. A., Bertetti, P., & Freeman, M. (2014). *Transmedia Archaeology: Storytelling in the Borderlines of Science Fiction, Comics and Pulp Magazines.* Springer.

The Marshall Project. (2014a). About. Retrieved October 3, 2019, from The Marshall Project website: www.themarshallproject.org/about

The Marshall Project. (2014b). Our People. Retrieved October 3, 2019, from The Marshall Project website: www.themarshallproject.org/people

The Marshall Project. (2014c). Our Supporters. Retrieved October 11, 2019, from The Marshall Project website: https://www.themarshallproject.org/ funders

The Marshall Project. (2018). Death Penalty in America: A Marshall Project Discussion Group. Retrieved October 11, 2019, from Facebook website: https://www.facebook.com/groups/445782675869683/?source_id=144278 5962603494

Veglis, A. (2012). From cross media to transmedia reporting in newspaper articles. *Publishing Research Quarterly , 28*(4), 313–324.

Ward, S. J. A. (2018). *Ethical Journalism in a Populist Age: The Democratically Engaged Journalist.* Rowman & Littlefield.

Weinreich, N. K. (2011). The Immersive Engagement Model: Transmedia Storytelling for Social Change. Retrieved October 1, 2019, from Weinreich Communications | Change for Good website: http://www.social-marketing. com/immersive-engagement.html

Zeiser, A. (2015). *Transmedia Marketing: From Film and TV to Games and Digital Media.* CRC Press.

Zelizer, B. (2004). *Taking Journalism Seriously: News and the Academy.* SAGE.

Zelizer, B. (2005). The Culture of Journalism. In M. Gurevitch & J. Curran (Eds.), *Mass Media and Society* (pp. 198–214). Bloomsbury Academic.

Zelizer, B. (2017). *What Journalism Could Be.* Polity Press.

# 4 The misty journey of independence

Firstly, we touched on where journalism in Turkey stands within the global context. For that, we followed a path that narrowed down from the global struggles of the news environment to the struggles of a specific geography, Turkey. Later, we introduced the notion of transmediality, in search of a perspective to understand this struggle. Chapter 3 has conveyed the scholarly understanding of transmediality from past to present. Starting with Jenkins' (2010) seven core principles of transmedia storytelling and moving along to Moloney's (2011) rendition of these principles to journalism practice, and then Canavilhas' (2013) common set of rules for fictional and nonfictional transmedia production to, lastly, Freeman's (Freeman, 2018b) value-laden perspective of transmedia ethos, we have passed through a tunnel of evolution to construct a framework of transmediality. For the final step of this research, this chapter sets out to use this framework on three different Turkish independent journalism initiatives. The aim behind this effort is twofold: looking through the lens of transmediality to study different cultures of independent journalism initiatives in Turkey and to investigate the role transmediality plays in these formations.

The three cases of interest for this research are Bianet (Independent Communication Network), Medyascope, and Ünsal Ünlü. The reasons behind choosing these cases are manifold. Firstly, they are initiatives that are born out of inadequacies within Turkish mainstream news media. Secondly, as they try to paddle their own canoes, they abstain from being the voice of a political party, company, organisation, or a religious network. Thirdly, they share a common belief, which is constructing a civil, independent, free, and pluralistic news media environment in Turkey. Fourthly, they form communities that share similar needs and desires within the world of news. As the fifth reason, they embody operational structures that are favourable for transmedia practices. Lastly, these cases provide diversity in the sampling with their differences in approach and execution.

For this research, I have conducted face-to-face interviews with the founders of the three initiatives. The rest of the chapter is mainly based on the information collected from these face-to-face interviews. In order to analyse these cases, we first look into how these initiatives came into play, what objectives they nourish at the present time, and how they carry out these objectives within the structure of their projects. Laying this information out beforehand helps us to position each case within the context of journalism in Turkey. Subsequently, based on the interviews, we approach these cases from the perspective of ethos and point out features that play a role in forming their communities. Lastly, we lay bare the pillars of sustainability for each case to paint the big picture of how these initiatives survive.

## The case of Bianet

On a Monday afternoon, I had the opportunity to sit down[1] with Nadire Mater[2] and talk about the independent journalism initiative she co-founded with Ertuğrul Kürkçü.[3] In fact, Bianet's story dates all the way back to almost 20 years ago. In other words, it was founded in a much different context than what we are in at the time of our interview. As Mater explains, the story of Bianet begins in the late 1990s. Having established a foundation—the IPS Communication Foundation[4]— to work within, Mater and Kürkçü had already focused on projects about strengthening the local media against the mainstream, raising the standard of ethically and politically responsible journalism. At the time, news media was again in a major crisis due to the merge of the media and the financial capitals in Turkey. Editorial independence in journalism was perishing, and people's right to information was forgotten (Bianet, 2011). The mainstream media scene including the local media, like today, was an arena of disinformation. Finding a news outlet to make your voice heard was a struggle for many segments of the society. Mater recalls that the spark of the Independent Communication Network (BIA) project actually appeared when the Union of Chambers of Turkish Engineers and Architects (TMMOB) could not find a mainstream news media outlet to announce its highly important studies on the energy crisis in Turkey. The union linked arms with the IPS Communication Foundation to establish its own news media agency and reach the public. Later on, Turkish Medical Association (TTB) joined this pursuit and the spark ignited into an independent network of collaboration and communication among small independent local media units, such as radio, television, newspapers, and websites (Bianet, 2011).

Bianet, which sustains today as the first and long-living independent news initiative of Turkey, was the primary outcome of the BIA project. It originally was an initiative of the local media that calls on solidarity on the basis of production and provides a space for anyone to add their own content to the common pool of knowledge, in forms of sound, image, or text. Sparking from the issue of energy crisis, Bianet expanded its focus across various titles in time, such as women, children, gender, Kurds, the poor, the unemployed and the labourer, in general, rights-based journalism. Mater points out to this evolution of focus as she explains:

> There was a page dedicated to business economy in the mainstream, but there were no pages spared for the topic of labour. With this type of reverse perspective, we asked ourselves whether it is possible to design a new media space.
>
> (N. Mater, personal communication,
> September 16, 2019)

As commercial benefits controlled the content and operations in mainstream media in Turkey, one of the solutions that came to mind was creating an independent media. It was the vision of a media that "renders the hegemony of social benefit [...] upon the material and financial tools of production and distribution of information in Turkey and internationally" (Bianet, 2011, para. 8). Bianet was not alone in its endeavour. The local media, independent newspapers, rights organisations, and academicians of communication were ready to collaborate in this formation of an alternative communication network (Bianet, 2011).

During our interview, Mater also emphasised on the areas where they thought it was necessary to blaze a trail. For the past 20 years, Bianet's pursuit of positive change through rights-based journalism involved developments regarding the Internet,[5] portrayals and the language in the news. Firstly, it is important to state that by the time Bianet was first launched, the Internet was a concept that was unknown to many. Mater recalls that before the Internet, they mainly used fax machines to distribute information and IP network-based communication channels within the office space. Until one day in 1997, a friend of a friend who worked in Microsoft at the time agreed to visit Istanbul to give an educational conference to explain what the Internet is and how it works. Mater proudly states that Bianet, as the organiser of this conference, became the pioneer of bringing awareness and importance of the Internet to the process of news making and, perhaps, cast the first stone in its search for a new media network. Secondly, Mater points out that not only in Turkey but also in journalism practices all over the world, there are still existent examples of stereotyped understanding of general definitions, such as gender-based journalism. In her example, Mater refers to the misconceptualisation of "gender equals woman, harassment and rape" (N. Mater, personal communication, September 16, 2019). What she suggests is to understand the concept of gender in its totality, including all of its segments, such as masculinity, femininity or LGBTQi+. In this sense, Bianet also blazes a trail with its attempt to dig out inaccurate portrayals frequently used in journalism practice and place them in their socio-political context. Lastly, Mater believes that language and how we use it is one of the most crucial problems of news making in Turkey and around the world as well. The incriminating, masculine, aggressive, militarist, and violent discourse that is used in present mainstream news is signalling the deterioration of news language. On that note, Mater reminds us about the pivotal role of language in the construction of governmental power. She positions careful and quality use of language at the centre of every news that is produced by Bianet.

### Structure

The initiative's interwoven multimodal structure branches out to various channels of communication to educate and practise on rights-based journalism. It also serves as an archive that documents invaluable information on rights-based issues through source books, news magazines, monitoring reports, special files, and other online database projects. However, the structure of Bianet has changed a lot over the years. Mater expresses how things change so quickly in many aspects of life in Turkey, especially in technological and legal sense. In order to draw the most up-to-date picture, this research is going to convey the initiative's structural information mainly from the personal interview with Mater and observations of Bianet's online and offline activities since 2017.

Starting from the educational perspective, Atölye BIA coordinates workshops, seminars, and other programmes with the support of the Swedish International Development Cooperation Agency (SIDA). These educational programmes are open to all journalists from different departments of the media, unemployed journalists, communication faculty students, and anyone who wants to practise journalism. They cover a variety of perspectives based on rights, gender and child-based journalism along with peace journalism, investigative journalism, judicial journalism, and more (Orman, 2019). Bianet's Instagram page shares images from these seminars and workshops (Bianet, 2018a). Although Atölye BIA has only become active in June 2018, the mentioned workshops and seminars have been a part of Bianet for many years under different titles. Mater sees this atelier a school, for which they travel all around Turkey to bring awareness on mentioned topics.

Out of the travels, seminars, workshops, and presentations over the years, along came the books of BIA library. Mater notes that they produced around 25 books that came out of the presentations and discussions thereafter. She also adds that these books still have an important place in the education of communication within academia. The books include many authors and many conflicting perspectives. Mater refers to these debates as the nature of pursuit, as she says, "There is not a single formula for journalism, that is why conflict is necessary when you are in search of a solution" (N. Mater, personal communication, September 16, 2019).

In its quest for independent and free media, Bianet also observes the course of events in the legal segment of Turkey. These observations are then documented as monitoring reports. The reports include titles relating to murdered and imprisoned journalists, active inquiries and trials, personal rights and compensation cases. Authored by Erol Önderoğlu,[6] the monitoring reports bring rights and freedom of expression violations of the media scene into view every three months and document each case in detail. By doing so, these reports contribute to the ongoing effort on fighting against these violations and archiving each case in detail.

As of 2019, a media monitoring database has been launched by Bianet with the support of the SIDA and the Heinrich Böll Stiftung Foundation (Bianet, 2019). This database archives the monitoring reports of Bianet, which have been published since 2017. It aims to provide an information centre where cases/interventions against media employees and institutions can be traced. It pieces together lawsuits and other legal, judicial, and administrative interventions regarding the freedom of expression of journalists and media institutions. Another database of interest within the structure of Bianet is an online library that focuses on the issues of gender in news making, which is titled as the Gender Based Reporting Library (Bianet, 2018b). This online library database came into existence with the support of the SIDA and European Instrument for Democracy & Human Rights

(EIDHR). It includes subsections of how-to guides, research analysis, news interviews, glossary, and resources. What it aims is to promote a journalistic approach that considers gender equality as a basic human right at every stage of news production (Bianet, 2018b). For that purpose, it serves as a source for journalists, media workers, and anyone who wants to work on gender-based journalism.

Since Bianet consists of multiple fragments of unique projects, it makes use of an online space, where all these fragments come together as a map of hyperlinks. *Bianet.org*, as the main website, acts as a hypertextual hub and directs its readers among online and offline news content relating to rights-based journalism. Within this website, one can read news articles or browse through images in the gallery. The "Special Files" section contains a selection of articles, photo interviews, audio recordings and reviews that were published on *Bianet.org*. In addition to Turkish content, the website gives place to Kurdish and English news articles that are specifically published for non-Turkish-speaking people. Bianet's online weekly news magazine, Biamag, is also a popular source of information. In it, people can find articles that include comments on daily developments, cultural and art news, events, and political debates (Bianet, 2011). The website hub presents hyperlink connections to the BIA library, the Gender Based Reporting Library, news about Atölye BIA, the Media Monitoring Database, and Bianet's social media accounts.

Last but not least, Bianet is an initiative that is active in social media platforms, such as Twitter, Instagram, Facebook, and YouTube. Through these social platforms, the initiative shares news articles from Bianet, event reminders of Atölye BIA, videos of interviews, launching of new projects, or letting people know about the latest monitoring reports. As Mater agrees, these platforms, especially Twitter, provide an interactive communication space between Bianet and its readers. Additionally, subscribers of Bianet newsletter can receive information on reports and events through their personal emails. This type of communication opens up an extra door to grab the reader's attention in the context of their daily routine.

### Ethos

Bianet, still to this day, gathers people in need of recognition within the society's complex fabric. The surrounding community of Bianet manifests in its social media spaces, events, and personal emails. The question of what binds this community together, perhaps, has many answers. However, in the context of journalism in Turkey, it is not farfetched to view this community as a crowd that shares common values of rights, including the right to information through quality journalism.

The shared values within Bianet's community encourage its readers and participators to follow its content from one medium to another. Mater believes that it is possible to pinpoint the size of this community as they show themselves in social media platforms, the main website and personal emails:

> We have a community, who reads our content very carefully and responds respectfully [...] There have been times when a single article has been read by 500,000 people. This is not a common occurrence, and in such situations, we cannot exactly figure out who these readers are. However, if an article is read by 2,000 people, it is easier for us to figure out who they are. They are a niche group.
>
> (N. Mater, personal communication,
> September 16, 2019)

Bianet, with almost 20 years of history, has built a rooted community that either has become a part of the initiative or continue to pursue the content that is produced daily. The shared values and beliefs also build the foundation of partnership with similar organisations, encouraging the community to follow other partnering projects.

### Sustainability

Collaboration with external organisations can be viewed as a pillar to sustain this initiative. However, it is not the only one. Along with collaboration, the initiative needs financial stability, adaptation to technological advances, and heightened engagement with the audience. In order to survive in the independent waters away from the mainstream, Bianet has been standing on international funds, partnering projects, its technological disposition, and high level of interactivity with its readers.

Bianet partnered numerous regional and worldwide projects over the years. An example of a national collaboration is a previously mentioned project, Media Ownership Monitor Turkey ("Who owns the media in Turkey," 2016). This project gathered Bianet and Reporters without Borders (RSF) together to unveil the unknowns of media ownership in Turkey. For this example, Mater adds: "I think that journalism with its pros and cons, problems and pleasures, all of it is worldly and universal. So, we need to share, understand each other, listen to each other" (N. Mater, personal communication, September 16, 2019). Being a part of international projects is also an invaluable asset in Mater's opinion. She believes that intercultural activities are key to understanding people who we usually are accustomed to call the "other." Although we all share similar fibres, we tend to contempt each other for our differences. Therefore, Mater clarifies how they actually value travelling internationally to share Turkey's side of journalism or inviting international journalists to share their journalism culture. These international gatherings offer new horizons to Bianet, where they meet journalists of the world. Solidarity that comes out of this collaboration can be priceless at times. As a case in point, on July 16, 2019, the Ankara Magistrate Judge decided to deny access to 136 URL addresses under a law that regards the protection of national security and public order.[7] One of the URL addresses listed in this decision was *bianet.org*. Although this caused a short-term panic, it did not take effect thanks to the supporters of Bianet from all around the world.

The initiative also values collaboration within its core structure. In fact, it acts as a mutual system of reinforcement. In order to clarify, Mater recalls how her discussions with Sevda Alankuş,[8] an academician of communication, shaped the way they define certain concepts in reporting, such as conceptualisation and theorisation of "right-based journalism," and "rights-based peace journalism," bringing concerns of the both together, although there is a claimed tension between them in theory. Additionally, Bianet is still in collaboration with lawyers who specialise in issues of rights. These experts bring invaluable experience and perspective to the table. Moreover, Mater also provides examples of how some of the readers send them articles to look at, which sometimes gets published and sometimes not. The reason for that is, as Mater states, all the published material on Bianet is subject to thorough editorial decision process, as they carefully consider the value of any submitted work. Hence, they do not mind taking the time to go through everything before it gets published.

Another aspect to investigate for sustainability is the financial stability. Mater states that in countries that are governed by some kind of democracy—countries that are mainly addressed as Western countries—there are public funds. These funds are precisely invented to be used in initiatives like Bianet. Turkey also has such a funding system, however, as Mater highlights, Bianet is unable to reach those public funds. Mater also underlines the problems of relying on funds with regard to sustainability. Since the doors of financial support are closed in Turkey, Bianet is left to seek support from international sources. Getting support from international sources sometimes attract critical attention from certain circles of the media. However, Mater adds that the owners of these funds never interfere in the content of Bianet or demand partisanship. Although the initiative gets motivational support from its community, getting financial support from its followers has never been brought into the open. Mater acknowledges the power of crowdfunding; however, she fears that the support from such channel may not be enough to sustain Bianet just yet. She also adds that a way to donate to the project can be, perhaps, possible in the near future.

When we look into Bianet's technological disposition for its sustainability, we can see that the initiative is making use of diverse and multiple communication channels to reach its readers. With contemporary media technologies offering countless possibilities of communication between the producer and the consumer, Bianet's disposition can be considered as timely to its surroundings. However, as change comes fast and efficient in the technological realm, keeping up with this change is a hard battle for Bianet. Mater is also aware of this fast pace of change and indicates that finding ways to stay up-to-date in their technological decisions is constantly in her mind.

Adapting to the advanced media technologies also brings about possible channels of interaction with the readers. Interactions come in many shapes for Bianet. Some come in forms of comments, some come in forms of articles and some as emails. In the case of comments, Mater believes they could be more harmful than beneficial. Although they receive some comments with respectful language, more often than not, they receive offensive comments. Mater also adds that there are two types of crowd in this game. On the one hand, there are the ones who feel such freedom and comfort to share whatever comes to their mind. On the other hand, there are the ones who feel such restrain that they cannot share any thoughts. In this unbalanced environment, interactivity through posting comments becomes a cautious subject for Bianet. Ruling out comments as a way of engagement might be a disadvantage; however, I would still consider this initiative to have the highest level of engagement because what Bianet offers its readers is a blank canvas that they can contribute to. In that sense, consumers of the initiative are actually prosumers who can share their work to be published and take a part in the cause. In return, prosumers become another pillar of sustainability for this initiative.

It is, in the end, all for the better. Sustaining Bianet, as Mater states, brings much responsibility to one's shoulders. However, she also adds, seeing the light at the end of the tunnel makes it all bearable. When a newspaper uses the phrase "male violence" instead of "violence against women" or when "peace journalism" begins to be spoken about and taught in universities, Mater understands that all the struggle is worth it. The motivational support to go on is not to be forgotten as Mater concludes: "Being a journalist is exhilarating, at the end of the day, it is documenting experiences, revisiting past events for the agenda and creating awareness" (N. Mater, personal communication, September 16, 2019).

## The case of Medyascope

Advances in media technologies have also been a source of influence for some journalists. Medyascope (Medyascope.tv), which was founded by Ruşen Çakır[9] in August of 2015, is a convenient example of such case of influence. The story behind Medyascope dates all the way back to the general elections held on June 7, 2015. During that time, Çakır became one of the first journalists to utilise Periscope's live broadcasting feature to convey his analyses on the elections to the public. Influenced by its ease of content production and distribution, Çakır used Periscope to broadcast his live programmes from his office in *Habertürk Newspaper*[10] or from election rallies. He also conducted interviews with the members of the Turkish Parliament and brought first-hand information right into the pockets of the public through Periscope.

What brought forward the existence of Medyascope was a collaboration between Çakır and two other people, Demet Tezel and Nurdan Üçer, who were partners in a firm that focuses on new media technologies. This collaboration sparked the idea of constructing a platform, where Çakır can share his Periscope programmes and other journalists can contribute. Hence, on August 20, 2015, Çakır sat down with two other colleagues in his office at *Habertürk Newspaper* and broadcasted the first open session programme of Medyascope. In time, this spark of an idea that started with three people in a small office flamed into a widely known initiative that has almost 40 permanent employees working in a large open workspace and a production studio. The initiative's main office was also the setting where I had the opportunity to meet and have a talk[11] with Çakır about the recent state of this independent journalism initiative.

Medyascope was born in a time when Turkish mainstream news media could not function properly due to political pressures, punishments, and censorship. Four years later, the contemporary function of the mainstream news media, perhaps, can be described as non-existent other than its use for governmental propaganda purposes. However, Çakır stresses that when Medyascope came to life, it did not come out as an act of resistance to the political pressure, or as an activism. In fact, he believes that approaching journalism from such a perspective can be harmful, as he states:

I do not prefer to see this as an act against the political power because that way of thinking puts a lot of responsibility on journalists' shoulders. That is a very poisonous situation. We are not positioned as activists here. People presume that our slogan, "Çünkü Özgürüz" (Because We Are Free), only refers to a stand against the political power, but it actually, at the same time, refers to a freedom against clickbait and rating based journalism. In other words, Medyascope was not a challenge against the government, but a way of distancing us away from the existent state of the news media in general.

(R. Çakır, personal communication, September 6, 2019)

According to Çakır, associating Medyascope with the problem of press freedom in Turkey is a misinterpretation. He prefers to evaluate this initiative as a result of the transformation of traditional news media into the digital realm. As he states in Medyascope's website (*medyascope.tv*), there is a need for a civil, independent, free, and pluralistic news environment in Turkey (Çakır, 2015). Traditional mainstream media fails to fulfil it, and social media offers a beneficial environment for the news to flow in civil, independent, free, and pluralistic manner (Çakır, 2015).

Considering the initiative, Çakır touches upon certain matters that Medyascope regards in its operation: practicing inclusive, participative, and pluralistic journalism; creative usage of new media tools; producing quality journalism; and being an alternative voice to mainstream news media. Firstly, what Çakır means by inclusive, participative, and pluralistic journalism is a news practice that covers diverse themes within a participative environment that is open to collaborators from any segment of society. Secondly, Çakır trusts the potential of technology and their necessity in constructing an alternative media space for quality journalism. He defines their mission as "combining conventional journalism practices with what new media technologies offers us" and "to practice quality journalism in its universal form" (R. Çakır, personal communication, September 6, 2019). As the third highlight, Çakır states that quality journalism is losing value in Turkey not only in mainstream media outlets but also in other independent news platforms, due to copy-paste journalism and disinformation. On that account, Çakır comments that practicing quality journalism is at the forefront in every decision they make in Medyascope. Lastly, Çakır explains Medyascope's first intention to cover areas where the mainstream media could not fill. However, as he admits, because mainstream media in Turkey is non-existent, Medyascope had to undertake that responsibility. Çakır describes this undertaking as follows:

> We may not want to be the mainstream. But we contain most of the criteria of being a mainstream [...] For example, we produce main news bulletin. Normally, Medyascope does not have to do something like that. But since the mainstream media in Turkey does not have a backbone, we were faced with such an obligation. Interestingly, however, when we started producing the main news bulletin, in time, it became our backbone.
>
> (R. Çakır, personal communication, September 6, 2019)

What Çakır mentions in this quotation contains a vital perspective, which is what this research builds a part of its foundation on. Medyascope could have just been another alternative news source in a context where mainstream news held its place and fulfilled its purpose. However, in contexts such as Turkey, where mainstream media is polluted and inadequate to the level that it is non-existent, alternative efforts are left with a responsibility to fill huge gaps. As the gaps get bigger and deeper, the alternative drifts apart from its definitional positioning and borrows traits from the mainstream.

### Structure

Then, how does Medyascope operate as an independent journalism initiative? Its operational structure consists of an interwoven multimodal structure that produces content for multiple media channels in various media forms. Just as in the case of Bianet, this research emphasises on the elements that are most prominent and talked about. The following paragraphs delve into some of these operational parts that exhibit Medyascope's transmedial disposition.

First, it is important to note that this initiative, in the beginning, was set out to function like a news TV channel, but in time, it branched out to other media channels. Its content is mostly video-based. When I ask Çakır the reason behind this decision, he simply replies: "To make a difference! There are so many sources that use solely textual material and most of them are copied and pasted from other sources and there is nothing new about it" (R. Çakır, personal communication, September 6, 2019). Gathering from Çakır's words, it is possible to imagine that, perhaps, the form of video, in this context, discourages the bad habit of copy-paste journalism and encourage production of distinct news content. Although the content they create is mostly video-based, the use of text and audio is also apparent as Medyascope publishes news articles and podcasts. Secondly, there are many individuals, groups, and organisations who provide content for Medyascope. It offers journalists, including those who have lost their jobs due to government pressure, a platform for uncensored journalism to reach a wider audience. While some of these external providers share large amount of content regularly (daily or weekly), some prefer to share a small amount irregularly.

As aforementioned, broadcasting live news programmes on Periscope is where Medyascope took its first step. This first step, actually, still to this day, continues to be the main feature of Medyascope. Every morning, the daily broadcast schedule is shared with the audience. People who find time in their daily routine to watch the live programmes, tune into Periscope, Facebook or YouTube. People who miss these live broadcasts, due to having busy working schedules, can access them later from the archive in the mentioned social media platforms or the main website. These programmes consist of content that is categorised under the titles of agenda, special programmes (sports, politics, business, society, world, culture), main news bulletin, and interviews. Additionally, there are programmes dedicated to commentary and analysis, including Çakır's own regular programmes. On that note, the Medyascope broadcast offers an extensive coverage of subjects, which renew daily.[12] In the absence of quality, diversity, and plurality in mainstream news, Medyascope aims to keep its practice alive by staying true to the universal standards of quality journalism.

Although its first steps were taken by means of video-based approach, this initiative also prioritises the form of mere sound to communicate with its audiences. Medyascope podcasts can be accessed through audio platforms, such as Spotify, Soundcloud, and iTunes platforms, as well as the main website. While most of these podcasts consist of repeated content from the live video broadcasts, some of the programmes within Medyascope only produce audio content from interviews, such as 2hafta 1gün (2weeks 1day).[13] Moreover, besides Medyascope's own podcast programmes, there is also room for collaboration with other podcast providers, such as Medyapod.[14] What these podcast platforms offer is not only an audio archive but also means to access content in restricted contexts. For instance, Çakır explains how some people prefer listening to the audio-based content as they are stuck in traffic, which is a very frequent and prolonged occurrence in the big cities of Turkey, especially in Istanbul. In a sense, Medyascope shows susceptibility to its audience's changing context during the day.

The initiative's website hub harbours all the news articles, news videos, and podcasts it produces or gathers from collaborators. The website builds hypertextual bridges among different media forms and channels, as well as different perspectives of a phenomenon within a network of information. Among video- and audio-based content, the website also contains textual material transcribed from video-based programmes or podcasts. Some of the content producers contribute to Medyascope through written articles.

Diversity of language is of particular importance for this initiative. Besides Turkish, the initiative offers news in English, Persian, and Kurdish. As Çakır states, they have recently started news programmes in French, and they will soon add content in German. This diversity offers several advantages to the initiative. Firstly, Çakır claims that there is a need for diversity in language, because there is a non-Turkish-speaking crowd out there, interested in what is going on in Turkey. He recalls that back in the day, if you lived abroad, you needed custom-ised satellite dishes to access content from your home countries' TV channels or remain limited to watching Turkey-based channels that were specially broadcasted in foreign countries, such as *ATV Europe*.[15] Nowadays, one does not need such struggles and limitations. It is possible to reach Medyascope content from anywhere in the world. Secondly, Çakır states that there are young collaborators working within the initiative, who are prone to different languages, willing to expand the linguistic borders of reach. Thirdly, Çakır emphasises on the prestige it brings to the work they do. He explains with the follow-ing words: "There is a great interest in Medyascope, especially in the West. Among people who are seriously interested in Turkey, there are very few people who do not know about us. For instance, diplomatic circles are aware of us" (R. Çakır, personal communication, September 6, 2019). Medyascope also received a prestigious ranking in the *FT Future 25: Middle East* report by the *Financial Times*, which was an-nounced in 2019 (England, 2019). In this report, Medyascope is among the 25 promising companies in the Middle East, creating a break in the sector and succeeding despite impossibilities in the region. It is also important to note that Medyascope is the only media organisation listed form Turkey.

Last but not least, remembering how it all started, Medyascope is an organisation that prioritises the effective use of social media channels. Stating from his own observations, Çakır claims that some of their followers first enter Medyascope's narrative through social media accounts such as Periscope, Facebook, YouTube, Instagram, or Twitter, especially in times of elections. In each of these social media platforms, it is possible to obtain different bits of information in different media forms, since each platform offers somewhat distinct means of communication. For instance, besides linking to live broadcasts and news posts, Facebook showcases the community of Medyascope and its audience reviews, along with a feature of "watch party" that some of the programmes prefer to use for interactive experience. Instagram delivers backstage photos of before or after programmes, in other words, memories of people who create Medyascope content. LinkedIn account shares information about Medyascope in its business context. This information includes who works in this platform full time and what accomplishments it has made. Twitter mainly acts as a channel of news distribution among the followers. In this social platform, hyperlinks and summaries of news content from the website hub are retweeted and commented on by the public. Lastly, as mentioned, Medyascope uses YouTube in its live broadcast sessions. However, this video-based platform also acts as a video archive for these live broadcasts.

### Ethos

Aside from reaching its audience among numerous media channels, Medyascope, on a deeper level, reserves certain beliefs and values in its circle of audience that encourage further participation to keep the initiative alive. The common belief in people's right to information; the shared value of a free, independent, and pluralistic media environment; and the need of an unrestricted, civilian, and pluralistic news media setting gather a loyal follower crowd around Medyascope.

The audience that mobilise with ethos show a heightened sense of engagement that not only encourages to follow the stories but also brings forward a supportive layer to the initiative. This supportive layer is visible in the following examples given by Çakır. Firstly, the monthly support collected from crowdfunding (Patreon) is an indicator. Çakır states that although the amount that is collected from crowdfunding is not extraordinary, it is clear to see a deep bond with a group of people who are willing to pay for a free service to keep it alive. In that sense, crowdfunding not only provides financial support but also a moral one. Secondly, the support of a crowd outside of Turkey is apparent. Çakır tells the story of an incident where they needed a specific technological device and a follower from abroad sent it to them which they used for three years. As Çakır states, people from abroad also visit Medyascope to give moral support when they come to Turkey. Another story he tells is about the time he went abroad to receive an award for Medyascope and how Turkish people in that event raised money among them. Çakır's last example involves the recent change in the initiative's logo. One day the publishing director of an online art platform (*artspeak.nyc*) in New York calls Çakır and asks if he could contribute to the initiative by designing a new logo for Medyascope. This new logo has been in use since 2019.

Medyascope, with its attention to the offerings of social media technologies, uses its multimodal structure to reach audiences everywhere in any context. However, its narrative structure is not the only factor in its audience's attachment to this initiative. What attracts and navigates its audience within its content also happens on a deeper level, the level of ethos. People who gather around this initiative share the common problem of a non-functioning mainstream news media and the lack of quality news all around the news environment of Turkey. Meeting under common values, followers of Medyascope engage with its stories, characters, and participate in its preservation.

## Sustainability

Although the loyal community of Medyascope is willing to give their moral and financial support, there is more help needed than meets the eye to sustain such an initiative. After all, as Çakır explains, it is trying to survive in a context where people who are holding the financial resources are keeping themselves distant due to the political conditions of Turkey. Therefore, making a profit becomes a struggle and even next to impossible. The collaboration among journalists and other organisations is, perhaps, another pivotal aspect that needs to be considered among ways of sustainability. Additionally, Çakır places emphasis on keeping the technological foundation of the initiative up-to-date and being receptive to the advances in the media environment. He is aware that each day comes with its innovative force and keeping up with the audiences' daily habits is one of the necessities for survival. Lastly, Çakır values the importance of sincerity and sacrifice in everything they do.

The financial extent of the project consists of various income channels. One of these channels is advertising and sponsorship. The website hub includes a detailed page on how one can sponsor a programme or place an ad. However, according to Çakır, this income channel falls inefficient because no one in the commercial realm prefers to give an advertisement due to the political climate. The second income channel is raising money through Patreon. On this crowdfunding platform, Medyascope has a monthly goal of $5,000 and it has reached a total amount of $4,203 with the support of 666 patrons (Medyascope, 2017). Çakır states that the support that is received from Patreon covers only a fractional part of their expenses; however, this platform is valuable since it allows them to see the bond they have with their followers. As the third and main income channel, the initiative receives funds from abroad through a private foundation (The Chrest Foundation) and other organisations (The Heinrich Böll Foundation Turkey Representation, The European Endowment for Democracy, Swedish International Development Cooperation Agency) (Medyascope, 2015). As Çakır admits, the funds that come in from these sources are mostly spent in the process. This is also why he is reluctant to call this financial plan a business model because there is no profit made yet. However, he adds, because they were successful in what they do, they had no difficulty in finding funds, which enabled their growth in time.

Over time, the strength and importance of collaboration also increased, earning a pivotal spot on the list of things that keep Medyascope alive. The growth is visible in a section of the website that is dedicated to the content providers, which includes journalists, columnists, academicians, students, non-governmental organisations, and many more. The initiative provides a platform for individuals and organisations who want to make their voices heard. Medyascope offers an opportunity to reach wider audiences. In return, these content providers bring content to the table from various areas of interest, such as citizenship,[16] law,[17] or children.[18] The collaboration, still to this day, influences the richness of the content and offers hope to experienced journalists who lost their jobs in the political wind. According to Çakır, collaboration within the initiative happens in any way, shape, or form:

> Some people prefer to come in and broadcast in our studio. Some of them prefer to send a link to their video or podcast for us to share. This happens not only in Turkey but all around the world. A collaborator is producing videos on popular music in Canada. Elsewhere, in the UK, two collaborators are making Podcasts about sports. When one does it, others see it, and they also want to collaborate.
>
> (R. Çakır, personal communication, September 6, 2019)

Another form of collaboration happens between the young generation of Medyascope, who are more familiar with the advanced media technologies, and the experienced journalists, who are more familiar with the conventional perspective of journalism. Considering the state of the news industry in Turkey, Medyascope is one of the few work-places that provide the experience of quality journalism to young jour-nalists. As Çakır admits, even though the salary rates are not high, some of them join the family while they are still students and later decide to stay permanently.

The young tech-savvy members are helpful in keeping the initiative's technological infrastructure up-to-date. It is, perhaps, possible to see this picture of solidarity as a representation of what Medyascope is trying to accomplish: combining conventional journalism practices with what new media technologies offers us. Medyascope pays much attention to sustaining quality journalism in communication spaces where people spend most of their time on daily. For this reason, one can cross paths with this initiative when listening to a playlist on Spotify, while watching an interview on YouTube, or following daily events on Twitter. However, keeping the technological perspective up-to-date is not everyone's strong suit. Çakır is aware of this hardship and values the young generation's experience for knowing where to reach the rel-evant crowd. Case in point, a survey about podcast-listening habits conducted by Podiolab,[19] reveals an increase in the number of listeners and concentration in their consumption habits (İbrişim, 2019). This interest provides a very high potential for both content producers and advertisers in the podcast industry of Turkey (İbrişim, 2019). With a proper timing, Çakır reveals that someone in the team, who has an interest in podcasting, is making an effort to add a podcast room to the Medyascope workspace. New ideas and additions to the initiative are constantly in motion to keep the pulse of the news media consumer behaviour.

As Çakır continues, another aspect that requires careful consider-ation and expertise is the notion of interactivity through these new social spaces of communication. It poses no difficulty for him to un-derstand that interactivity, especially nowadays, is a vital part of the news environment. There is more than one way to participate within the narrative of Medyascope. One of them relates to people having the means to share their opinions on issues or ask for answers to their own questions. However, as also mentioned in the case of Bianet, these participative areas of communication have both advantages and disadvantages. While the advantages cover the construction of productive environments of discussion, the disadvantages can drag these discussions into acts of defamation, hate speech or even death threats. These demoralising comments do more harm than good for the content producers and the audience. Çakır admits that they were not able to form an effective system to manage the interactivity through comments yet and, for now, they prefer to leave the comments section closed for most of their live programmes. However, commenting is enabled under the posts of Medyascope's social media accounts. The "watch party" feature of Facebook is also available in some of these posts where groups can hold a live screening of pre-recorded videos. This feature offers a shared viewing experience by allowing all the group members to watch the content at the same time and all the while share their comments. Additionally, as in the case of Çakır's own commentary and analysis programmes, previously shared audience comments can generate a response from the programme producer and become part of the programme. Increase in the level of interaction can be observed as the community of followers participate in the financial stability of Medyascope. One of the factors that may have determined this increase is building up the trust within society towards what they do, and how they do it. Sharing backstage scenes of programmes on Instagram, delivering original news content on many forms or places and offering visibility to the invisible are, perhaps, some of the many reasons that gradually built up that trust. As Çakır indicates, from the beginning, this initiative was planned to progress through sincerity and sacrifice. He believes that this idea, still to this day, pays off a great deal in the initiative's existence and success. At the very beginning, as Çakır recalls, not many believed in what Medyascope could accomplish. People were too quick to disregard its aim and method. However, in time, with the deep level of connection and dedication of its community, Medyascope became one of the very few initiatives that poses hope for the future of quality journalism in Turkey.

## The case of Ünsal Ünlü

Up until now, we examined two independent journalism initiatives that are represented by a group of people working together to produce quality news to the public. This following case differs from the previous two cases because it is an initiative carried out by an individual who practises opinion journalism based on news analysis. As Ünsal Ünlü[20] and I sit down for a conversation at a coffee shop in Ankara,[21] he shares the context and objectives behind his initiative that he named as "Patron kızar mı?" demeden... (Without saying "Would the boss be mad?"). For the sake of clarity, this title is shortened as "Patronsuz" for the rest of this chapter. Ünlü is a journalist who has worked alongside issues regarding politics most of his career. He was dismissed from his position in the mainstream after a career of 25 years working as economics, prime minister, and presidential correspondent. As he states, what has dragged him to start this independent initiative is not his dismissal of his position but, actually, the dismissal of diverse opinions against and criticism towards the ruling government within the mainstream media domain. The ruling governments trying to take possession of the mainstream media is not a new phenomenon in the history of Turkish politics. However, Ünlü states that this transformation happened in such severity and speed that it was an obvious act of "revenge." What Ünlü refers to is a grunge that has been accumulated for years against the old ruling powers that had ignored and excluded the values of conservative segment. This comeback was going to happen by means of the mainstream media and, as Ünlü adds, the government was determined to form its own by reconstructing the existing one.

Pondering over how to go about with this project, Ünlü emphasises on three objectives that still underpin his vision. The first reason, similar to the cases of Bianet and Medyascope, is to construct a new media space where journalism can survive. It is a space that is free of restrictive bosses and governmental regulations. Ünlü believes that when this space is constructed, people will respond because, as he states, "necessity is the mother of invention" (Ü. Ünlü, personal communication, August 23, 2019). The second reason is the common interest of the public's right to information. Ünlü believes that the current state of mainstream media deprives the public of its right to not only factual information but also any information. To this respect, whether it is small segments or large segments of society, right to information is the common interest of all people. The third reason of this initiative involves healthy communication between individuals of the public as a method of conflict resolution. As mentioned in Chapter 2, the polarised state of the news media in Turkey also has an influence on Turkish society. Debating about politics has become such a sensitive matter that it more often than not ends in offensive behaviour between friends or even family members. Reintroducing tolerance to such an intolerant crowd is not an easy task. Although it may not happen in an instant, Ünlü believes that reminding people of what they have in common regardless of their differences can pave the way to a more tolerant and open-minded society.

### Structure

In view of these facts, when Ünlü started this initiative, he cared much about the friendly and warm atmosphere provided by Periscope's live broadcast feature. He also cared much about his audience's preferences and geographical context. His careful estimations led him to reshape and enhance the structure of Patronsuz to what it is today: an integrated storytelling structure with multimodal and interactive features.

Every weekday morning, at exactly 9:00 AM, Ünlü goes live on Periscope for 30 minutes to analyse and discuss the agenda of the day. His analysis involves choosing a specific subject to talk about and integrate it through various connection points to the daily agenda. Ünlü explains his reasoning with an example:

> When talking about wildfires, whether you like it or not, the issue leans against nepotism in Turkey. You have to talk about that because our Minister of Forestry is a man who has a Doctoral degree from a university, where his older brother is the Rector. No one else can give that degree to him. You must talk about this. This also brings forward certain political inheritances. You are obliged to explain the matter of political heritage in Turkey.
>
> (Ü. Ünlü, personal communication, August 23, 2019)

For these first live sessions of the day, Periscope provides a statistical average of 7,000 people who tune in at 9:00 AM. Perhaps, some of them are on their way to work, getting ready to start the day or in another country getting ready to go to bed. As Ünlü states, the consistency to start at 9:00 AM has a detailed thought behind it. Along with having 16 newspapers to read each morning before the sessions, Ünlü also takes global time differences on board and arrange his timings in accordance with a global audience.

After the first agenda setting live session that lasts until 10:00 AM, Ünlü goes live once again for the next live session at 10:30 AM on Periscope. This next live session lasts for an hour, where Ünlü goes through the newspapers of the given day to analyse "what these newspapers can and cannot write," which is also the title of these sessions. In addition to news analysis, Ünlü offers an educational perspective towards media literacy and criticism. As Ünlü emphasises, it is a necessity for this initiative to have a section dedicated to newspapers, because, among many of its definitions, a journalist is a person who deals with things that an ordinary person cannot reach for reasons such as lack of time and money. Therefore, bringing the newspaper to the public is an important part of this initiative.

These two consecutive live sessions were not always separate. In the initial sessions of Patronsuz, Ünlü produced daily single long sessions that first started with the agenda setting and moved on to the newspapers. However, as time went by and as the viewer statistics presented more accurate results, Ünlü realised that the content relating to agenda setting and the newspaper browsing had separate viewer profiles. Some people only want to know what is on the newspapers and some already know what is on them and only want to hear about Ünlü's analyses. Therefore, considering the contextuality, the previously long single session is now separated into two distinct sessions that serve different audiences.

In addition to daily agenda setting and news analysis, Ünlü also offers monthly Q&A sessions, where he first delivers a brief monthly report on the initiative's operational structure (viewer statistics, general state of income, and technological developments) and later chats with the audience through suggested questions. He describes these sessions as heart-to-heart discussions and titles them as "Serbest Uçuş" (Free Flight). These monthly discussion sessions are surely effective in increasing the interactivity degree of the initiative; however, Ünlü also cares about their potential to comfort the audience to share more and, perhaps, collectively clear their heads of a single agenda.

Within these sessions, the audience is also directed to different sources. Whether it be a news article, a social media post, or a recently published book, Ünlü integrates hypertextual links within his talks to expand the audience's storyworld. For instance, Ünlü's book recommendations are weekly occurrences in his live sessions. He states that whether he likes the book or not, if the book is related to the contemporary context, he recommends it. He also emphasises that recommending these books have no commercial or any other purpose other than directing people to read.

The initiative's offline expansion goes further than the recommended books. In various occasions, Ünlü conducts seminars and talks about issues relating to his initiative, such as transformation of media,[22] news and psychology,[23] and the relationship between conscience and consciousness.[24] During our interview, he also recalls a recent event[25] where he had the opportunity to spend time with more than 200 followers for what was planned to be an hour ended up lasting more than five hours.

While there is the apparent segment of followers asking questions and interacting with Ünlü's stories, there is also the private, hidden segment that prefers to interact through personal emails or WhatsApp messages. These private messages and emails portray a sense of sincerity that offers comfort to some followers who fear and hesitate to share their thoughts publicly. Some of Ünlü's examples of such private correspondence belong to the people who support the ruling government and even work within its executive positions. As Ünlü admits, these private chats do not form a centre of synergy, however, for him, they prove that this initiative is encouraging people from all segments to ask questions and criticise if necessary.

Since 2015, Patronsuz has strengthened its position and objective through series of broadcasted videos, events, and recommendations. After its four-year journey, it now gains the attention of 100,000 people daily (Ünlü, Streamed live on October 24, 2019). This number has grown gradually over the years. While some people, including me, have become aware of it through close friends, some have learned about it through news articles, some from social media posts. All these doors open to the initiative's main website (*unsalunlu.com.tr*). In this website, one can browse through the archived video programmes, articles, and book recommendations. In addition, under the section "Omuz Verenler" (Supporters), Ünlü shares a list of names who, one way or another, has supported the initiative. The main website hub also includes links to the initiative's social media accounts.

The initiative utilises each social media platform in different ways. As aforementioned, Ünlü broadcasts his morning live sessions on Periscope, and as of October 2019, these live sessions are also concurrently broadcasted on YouTube. At the beginning of these sessions, the viewers are asked to share the link of the broadcast on their social media accounts, calling others to join in. Immediately after each session, Ünlü uploads these sessions on YouTube as video and shares them on Facebook and Twitter. The audio versions of the sessions are also uploaded on Soundcloud and iTunes platforms. People who don't have time to catch the live performances in the morning can watch them on YouTube and Periscope or listen to the recordings on Soundcloud or iTunes on their way back home from work stuck in traffic. These uploaded files also serve as an invaluable archive of published newspapers and daily agendas of the last four years, providing useful data for further academic research. The morning sessions are not the only content that is shared on social media accounts. Ünlü frequently shares and retweets posts about news articles from external sources on Twitter. Some of these tweets brief the followers on how to support independent journalism initiatives alike. He also shares hashtags of cultural and other events that call for awareness and solidarity. Ünlü's Twitter account, with its many participative followers, provides a useful arm that reaches thousands of people and more (Ünlü, 2009). Instagram, however, paints a different picture about Ünlü's life. Among the photos shared on this platform, we can get a glimpse of his private life with his friends, cultural activities, leisure moments; or of his professional life, through scenes from his seminar talks, award shows, and other events. Instagram, perhaps, presents the sincerest picture of Ünlü's character within this storyworld.

*Ethos*

Ünlü, in our interview, often emphasised the importance of sincerity within his initiative. Sincerity, according to Ünlü, plays a major role in grabbing people's attention and drawing them together, especially in a time when it becomes harder and harder to find that honesty even in close proximity. This belief clearly manifests not only in his social media profiles but also at the opening and the concluding remarks of his live sessions. As he opens with the same remarks in each programme, he invites the audience to leave their biases behind and be ready to only talk for and about their country. To emphasise on the diverse texture of his global audience, he greets them with the language spoken in whichever geographical context they reside in. Later, at the end of each programme, he concludes with the ending remarks that emphasise their differences regarding political views, views on life, upbringing, ethnicity or sexual orientation. However, he adds that these differences have no power on their dreams for Turkey, as they all long for living in this country with better conditions.

What Ünlü observes from the audience feedback is that there are four visible consensus points where people start to gather around. First of all, as Ünlü explains, the hope was fading for the journalism in Turkey and with this initiative people understood that journalism is still possible. Secondly, the ability to talk with one another, regardless of differences, is put back on the table. People who used to cast others out for wearing a headscarf or being from the opposing political party are now learning to communicate and understand their commonalities. Thirdly, people started to loosen their strict bonds to their political parties. For this point, Ünlü gives an example of the August 2019 wildfire in Karabağlar, Izmir, which is one of the major cities in Turkey's west coast. He states that during that incident, people realised that the forest under fire did not belong to any political party, it belonged to the people of Turkey. Lastly, people began to conquer their fear. Fear, as also mentioned in Chapter 2, is one of the major factors of people losing trust and hope on the political system. Ünlü claims that this initiative plays an effective part in fading that fear away. He was able to observe it through the feedback he received from many political agents stating his positive influence on the high turnover in the local elections held on March 31, 2019. It is crucial to state that this success takes place despite the ignorance towards his existence by his journalist counterparts of the mainstream due to the same fear.

All these points of consensus did not form overnight. Patronsuz conveyed its messages regularly through live performances, social media posts, books, audio recordings, and seminars throughout its four-year journey and continues to do so. These messages of a better future, unity, and critical thought has formed a close-knit community within the initiative's operation, showing themselves in events or through their support. As a case in point, Ünlü recalls a moment when he was giving a talk in one of the seminars and he realised that there was a group of 30 people who already knew each other from the online space and organically formed a physical community in real life.

### Sustainability

The dedication is also visible in the collaborative efforts of his audience and other independent journalism initiatives alike. Ünlü believes that the collaborative effort of solidarity is the sole remedy to overcome the struggles we are facing today, as he expresses "There is an organised evil in front of us. We have no choice but to come out of it with an organized goodness. In the face of such evil, individual effort is useless. You need an organised community" (Ü. Ünlü, personal communication, August 23, 2019). Ünlü also states that Patronsuz has only reached to where it is today with the support of its followers. These followers collaborate with the initiative in many different aspects. For instance, in 2017, one of his followers made an effort to draw up an advertising sector data report of the main website for free. Through this report, Ünlü was able to learn valuable information about his audience, such as their demographics and consumption behaviours. Lacking the financial capability to obtain such information, Ünlü acknowledges the power of collaboration in this example. Another incident he recalls is about the upsetting comments intentionally shared by people to provoke or discourage others. Ünlü recalls a follower from Hungary who disclosed these trolls during one of his live sessions, preventing them to disrupt the flow of conversation any further. The collaboration happens not only between Patronsuz and its followers but also between the initiative and other independent journalism initiatives alike. Medyascope, for instance, supports Ünlü's programmes by sharing them on its main website and announcing them on its social media accounts. This collaboration brings advantage to reaching more viewers and expanding the borders of the story being told.

Contributions of followers do not only motivate but also support the initiative financially, helping it to survive within difficult conditions. Money, however, is a sensitive issue for a journalist and sometimes can get ahead of the purpose of the project. This also holds true for most independent journalism initiatives, as is also observed in the previous two cases. For his initiative, Ünlü lays out a system of income from various channels. The first income flows through a crowdfunding channel, Patreon. According to Ünlü, crowdfunding is actually cut out for this initiative because it comes forward with the claim of operating without a boss. However, he is concerned that the income coming from this source might get ahead of the actual purpose, which would influence the overall cause of Patronsuz in a bad way. For this reason, Patreon is also a cut out platform because it has an option to only specify the number of patrons one would like to reach. As of October 2019, with the goal of 10,000 patrons, the initiative has 655 patrons monthly contributing to the initiative (Ünlü, 2016). Although the earnings coming from Patreon is not in large amounts, as Ünlü admits, it is more important to know that such an alternative income channel is possible and that there is a supporting community within. The second income channel is through means of advertisement on the main website's homepage. Although this channel exists, it has the similar struggle Medyascope faces with finding candidates who are willing to be a part of this initiative. However, the "Supporters" page of the website operates in a similar fashion to placing an ad as the third income channel of this initiative. The names listed on this page, as Ünlü states, are legally treated as advertisements of these individuals who supported the initiative one way or another. The fourth channel is the advertisement income coming in from YouTube videos. Since these videos have high viewer counts, Ünlü receives up to $300 of monthly income from these videos. In order to increase his earnings from YouTube, Ünlü aims to reach the benchmark of 100,000 subscribers in the near future. On closer inspection, all of the income channels that are mentioned in this paragraph, up until now, are provided by the audience. Whether it may be the crowdfunding, name listing or YouTube advertising income, Ünlü is aware that the constant supporters of this initiative are its followers. Lastly, in 2019, the initiative received a fund from a collaborative project called Media for Democracy.[26] This fund is given to a selection of independent journalism initiatives to support their innovative projects. As Ünlü (2019) states in his free flight session on October 25, 2019, this fund was only used to improve the technological foundation of the initiative.

Technological infrastructure of Patronsuz is another major pillar of its sustainability. According to Ünlü, contemporary media technologies provide both the freedom to reach a wide audience from any place in the world and the limitless interaction paths for that audience to participate from anywhere. However, advances in technology are not always problem solvers; in fact, they can cause new issues to consider.

As Ünlü explains, there is a large segment of viewers who are above the age of 60. Although not all, some of these people struggle with handling smartphones and adapting to social media platforms such as Periscope. Ünlü admits that he is careful in the way he expands his storyworld to other media channels due to his older viewers. Moreover, it is important to point out that he also admits to his own lack of technological knowledge. As the technological infrastructure for broadcasting improves constantly, Ünlü feels the need of an update mechanism, who is his son. Gaining advantage from his experience with social media, Ünlü's son introduces his father to the significant issues he may face along the way, such as bots and trolls. Ünlü, realising the graveness of such issues, multitasks by moderating the live comments while he broadcasts. Most of the time he blocks the owners of the offensive comments. In extreme cases of threats or defamation, he files a criminal complaint with the prosecution. However, this type of close moderation by an individual is only possible in a single channel. As the initiative spreads out to multiple channels, the moderation of comments gets harder and eventually it limits the degree of interactivity. For instance, on October of 2019, Ünlü started to broadcast his sessions on YouTube and Periscope simultaneously. Failing to moderate the YouTube live stream chat space, Ünlü decided to turn it off.

Nevertheless, for Ünlü, interactivity is the most important part of this initiative's operational structure. As Ünlü expresses, "experiencing the immediate reaction of the viewers is the warmest connection you can have with them" (Ü. Ünlü, personal communication, August 23, 2019). These immediate reactions can sometimes act as a verification system for Ünlü. On many occasions, he recalls to being corrected or reminded by his audience on specific names, dates or updates on news. He adds that encouraging people to participate in the conversation is a battle that depends on the issue of trust. According to him, gaining that trust requires sincerity and patience. Every morning he sits in front of a microphone and calls out to his audience from his private home office. This setting, as Ünlü states, is intentional. It intends to portray a sense of intimacy through amateur choices of space and media. Ünlü believes that this amateur setting can provide comfort to the audience, leaving their fears of expression behind and share. Additionally, Ünlü uses humour as a method of persuasion and comfort. "To be able to laugh together" is what he finds significant to be sincere (Ü. Ünlü, personal communication, August 23, 2019). Pointing out a ridiculous situation together can make people much more comfortable. In fact, Ünlü believes that there is a well-established tradition of political satire in Turkey and Turkish political climate is a treasure for it. In such a case, humour becomes a method that brings people together and intensifies the degree of engagement. Moreover, as another form of expression, Ünlü reads poems within his video sessions to take the audience away from the political atmosphere. His hope is to introduce poems to people's daily lives as a way for them to realise that there is more than politics to cherish out there in real life. These poems also act as entry points to the stories told on online sessions. As Ünlü claims, some of the viewers join in just to listen to the poems but along the line they prefer to stay and get more information.

At the end of the day, what motivates Ünlü to keep on with this initiative is seeing signs of change in people's minds as they start to question and react to news flowing around them. These indications can be observed when a government official pours out his grief in a private email or when the viewers reconcile among each other within the comments section of live sessions. As Ünlü concludes, all he wants is for people to extract something, not everything at once but in bits and pieces, from the poems, books, seminars, and sessions. Perhaps, people can start to imagine that survival of journalism is still possible, when there is sincerity, modest technological infrastructure, and a community of participative supporters.

## The transmedial mesh of survival

All the three independent journalism initiatives have stories that are distinct from each other. As explained under the case titles, their objectives, ethos, operational structures, and plans of sustainability display different perspectives and details. More than two decades ago, Bianet set its path to practise rights-based journalism to fill the gap of news making regarding minorities. Medyascope rolled up its sleeves to save the deteriorating image of journalism in the mainstream domain and online spaces. Moreover, Ünsal Ünlü came forward to invite a polarised society to participate in a reconciliatory dialogue again. However, these cases also share various commonalities. Although emerged in different moments in time, they share a common point of origin, which is the inadequacy or absence of Turkish mainstream media in providing news to the public. This gap leads journalists, who advocate the right of the people to receive information, to consider alternative ways.

Within their operations they commonly utilise a different way of storytelling. It is a type of narrative which clearly shows similarities that correspond to Canavilhas' (2013) characteristics of transmediality. Through levels of interactivity, bridges of hypertextuality, various

forms of integrated multimodality and adaptations of contextualisation, all of the three cases offer immersive journeys to the world of
news. Firstly, for the sake of interactivity, in the cases of Bianet and
Medyascope, we observe audiences becoming authors or sometimes
editors, as they experience the highest sense of engagement. Ünlü's
live Q&A sessions position his audience at the centre of the initiative, giving them a sense of belonging to the cause. Secondly, all of
the three initiatives construct a network of information, which utilises
hypertexts and links to connect the fragments of their stories together.
For instance, while Bianet takes its audience from a news article to
an archival database and then a book, it gradually introduces new information and contexts to the reader. Ünlü takes advantage of this hypertextual space to expand his audience's horizons. He directs them to
external resources of information through his social media posts and
live sessions. Moreover, hypertextuality in Medyascope builds bridges
between institutions and organisations. It allows the audience to meet
new developments within the fabric of society. Thirdly, if we recall
Lemke's (2009, 2010) definition of these migrating audiences, in all of
the cases above, traversals are offered media-specific representations
of storyworlds that exist in narrative cohesion. As a case in point, while
Ünlü tries to construct feelings of sincerity and trust, he makes use of
multimodality through his amateur-looking live sessions and Instagram photos. Although the media forms he uses allow different ways
of representation, his promise of sincerity is embedded cohesively in
all of them. A similar situation is apparent in the cases of Bianet and
Medyascope. Bianet's multimodal structure of projects and contexts
offer different views of meaning-making regarding issues of minorities, gender, and children. The initiative, however, stays cohesive with
its general focus on rights-based journalism. Medyascope also gathers different media forms (live programmes, news articles, podcasts)
together. In addition, it also works with different institutions under
its umbrella. While each of these media forms and institutions offer
distinct representations within storyworlds, Medyascope presents
a cohesive picture as it preserves its practice of quality journalism.
Lastly, contextualisation is a trait that the cases directly apply in their
operation. Medyascope and Ünlü are the two cases that clearly adapt
specific content to fit the audience's daily routine, especially during the
times of morning and evening rush-hour traffic. Medyascope offers
various forms and languages of content while Ünlü adjusts the timing
of his live sessions according to the routine of his global audience.
It is also possible to state that Ünlü's use of humour and poems in
his stories can be seen as ways of contextualisation adapted to users'

consumption habits, dragging the consumer's attention to content and sparking curiosity and interest. Bianet, on the other hand, offers personalisation of content through its subscription services. Subscription to Bianet opens up a new entrance to the story as one receives personal emails to the initiative's developments such as reports and workshop invitations.

All of these efforts place the power of the narrative to the forefront to trigger an emotional response from the public. Bianet, Medyascope, and Ünsal Ünlü try to construct influential narrative representations of complex issues that Turkey faces within its journalistic milieu. Ünlü's efforts of sincerity, Medyascope's attention to pluralism and Bianet's collaborative practices are effective ways to evoke the public's desire to act and make the extra effort to support communities outside of their own. For this reason, they offer immersive experiences to reach their audience on a more emotional level. Transmediality, in this respect, plays an important role in these three cases, as they all use ubiquitous media outlets, allow their audiences to become prosumers and participate in the expansion of the story. Along the way, one can observe change happening through these initiatives. We can remember Mater's joy when she reads the correct wording of an event in the newspaper, "male violence," or Ünlü's appreciation when he receives an open-hearted email from a government official. Little by little, and with great patience, these independent journalism initiatives encourage the audience to participate, feel a sense of belonging to the story and extract something that they can apply to their own lives.

The heightened sense of engagement gathers communities that share common beliefs and values around these initiatives for support. The people who follow Bianet, Medyascope, and Ünlü are in search of trustworthy, inclusive, and investigative news. In their pursuit, they come together to question the existing state of journalism in Turkey. The bond they share is, perhaps, through what Yılmaz (2018) defines as the politics of desire. Besides the power of collaboration, these communities grow and gain strength through transmedia ethos, which plays a vital role in the existence of these independent journalism initiatives. Ünlü's community shows its support as they follow his live sessions each morning, attend his seminars for extended hours and finance the initiative through the crowdfunding platform, Patreon. The followers of Medyascope also demonstrate their appreciation through crowdfunding but, at the same time, by tuning into its live programmes on Periscope, volunteering for help and sharing its content in their social media platforms. Furthermore, Bianet's niche community, aside from distributing its articles and reports on social media, stands behind it in case of a threat to its existence.

It is possible to consider that these gatherings rise out of a cultural bond, recalling what Freeman (2018a) defines as cultural alternativism. In the absence of mainstream media, these initiatives form alternative cultures. We can observe within the stories of these initiatives that communities follow content that responds to their beliefs and values. It is through this line of thought that one may reconsider Ünlü and Çakır's argument of becoming the mainstream. Under excessive regulations and constant political propaganda, Turkey's mainstream news environment fails to represent the majority of Turkish society. Communities that follow Bianet, Medyascope, and Ünsal Ünlü are in search of news that represent their culture. The gap of cultural representation within the mainstream has grown to such an extent that the alternative initiatives feel the pressure to fill its place. Medyascope's production of main bulletin news programmes is a good example to this statement.

In this respect, within the context of journalism in Turkey, transmedia ethos not only assist in forming alternative cultures but also help to preserve the mainstream culture of journalism.

Sustaining the culture of journalism in Turkey has become an experimental journey to find new grounds to stand on. Considering the information gathered from the interviews, there are five distinct grounds that require attention: (1) Building an independent ownership structure, (2) partnering with nonpartisan organisations, (3) intensifying the engagement with the public, (4) preventing the distribution of disinformation, and (5) adapting to the digital age of global communication and social network. In each of these layers, we come across influences of transmediality that support the survival of these three initiatives.

Recalling the discussion on Chapter 2 about the ownership of mainstream news media in Turkey, it is the first and foremost canon of these three initiatives to stay independent of any partisan organisations. Independence, however, comes with its financial challenges, especially in Turkey, where your political position plays a major role in opening or closing doors of support from government and commercial sectors (advertising). For this reason, in pursuit of building their own independent ownership structures, Bianet, Medyascope, and Ünsal Ünlü are left to receive support from international funds and crowdfunding. However, trying to be freed of unethical and oppressive journalism environment, the three initiatives place their objectives and stories in front of their financial struggles. As they all express, these financial endorsements are the outcome of an ever-growing success that is determined by their communities. In that case, one could consider the formation of such communities to be the key to these initiatives' sustainability of independence. Therefore, it is not far-fetched to observe transmediality, and especially transmedia ethos, as one of the major influences in forming these communities, hence supporting their independence. By placing the power of the narrative at the forefront and helping to build a participative community of solidarity among individuals, transmediality acts as a supporting pillar of survival for these journalism initiatives.

The notion of solidarity does not only manifest through the audiences but also through partnering with nonpartisan organisations. When we closely observe these three cases, we can see a support system that operates through collaboration. Within this system, the initiatives get together with organisations to either receive financial support or expand their content. For instance, Bianet's collaboration with the German section of Reporters Without Borders (RSF) in the Media Ownership Monitor Turkey project, helps to expand Bianet's storyworld, raise awareness of the initiative and widen its scope of audience. Another example can be set forward about numerous organisations producing content within Medyascope's storyworld. These organisations add diversity not only to the content of the story but also to the representation of communities. Connections such as these examples are possible by allowing decentralised authorship within the storyworld and hypertextuality among the stories of these different authors. In this respect, having these two traits in its character, transmediality, again, plays an important part as a storytelling method that innately supports decentralisation and networking among multiple content creators.

Another canon of survival for these initiatives is to accomplish what they have set out to do: encourage the public towards action and positive change. As discussed in Chapter 3, journalists' responsibility as agents of social change in politics, economy, culture, and everyday life gives this practice its powerful essence. In order to steer the public in the direction of positive change, journalists need to find ways to convey their messages on a deeper level. A closer interaction with the audience in the news production and distribution processes is possible with contemporary media technologies. However, considering the three cases we observed, this interaction is not only possible but also necessary in the context of independent journalism in Turkey. The close interplay between the journalists and the public can be seen as one of the ways to gain back the lost trust towards journalism in Turkey. It can also open doors to a peaceful communication among the politically polarised Turkish society, leading the way to democratic public discourse. Therefore, by providing high to low degrees of engagement within their transmedia storyworlds, Bianet, Medyascope, and Ünsal Ünlü build participative news environments where sincerity rebuilds trust, people can express their opinions without fear, learn to respect the opinions of others, and form social communities. In all three cases, this engagement intensifies through multiple media channels, encircling the audience in an immersive experience. Transmediality, in this sense, with its promise of interactivity and audience performance, is a supportive method for journalists, namely, the agents of social change. Additionally, as change is a work of many, transmedia ethos helps to gather communities under one roof, ready to act when necessary.

Let's not forget, social change is only possible through careful collection, analysis, interpretation, definition, and reporting of accurate information. In other words, it requires thorough investigative work of facts done by journalists with qualified analysation skills. However, it is also not an easy task for these qualified journalists to deal with disinformation that spreads very quickly and easily in the contemporary news environment. Bianet tries to overcome this problem by giving more time to the editorial process of news production. Medyascope, to avoid the same issue, stays away from news reporting that leaves short time for verification, such as breaking news. Additionally, more often than not, experts and witnesses are invited as programme guests to obtain accurate first-hand information on a given subject. Furthermore, Ünsal Ünlü spends hours in preparation for his live sessions each day, doing research on the daily agenda and newspapers. What all of these initiatives have in common, which is also embedded in the fabric of transmediality, is that they prioritise the content of their stories rather than their speed of production. Thereafter, in case of faulty or broken information, the audiences are there to pick up the pieces. This is yet another practice that manifests within transmedia narratives. In all three cases, we can catch sight of audience participation to become a part of the fact-checking process. Through comments received in personal emails, under articles, social media posts, and during live chats, audiences can be seen to correct, add on or verify information. However, it is also important to state that the moderation and verification of these comments flowing from multiple interaction points are still issues discussed in media and journalism studies (see Diakopoulos, 2019; Eldridge & Franklin, 2018; Frischlich, Boberg, & Quandt, 2019; Ziegele, 2019).

The survival of journalism in Turkey, outside of the mainstream, also lies in efficient use of contemporary media technologies. All three initiatives are aware of the challenges these technologies bring forward and how journalism, as a practice, is falling behind in adapting to them.

They also express the difficulty and pressure of constant demands of enhancements in their ways of storytelling. The common agreement among Mater, Çakır, and Ünlü is that the young generation have different views on how news should be told, and journalism needs to adapt to this change to survive. For this reason, Bianet is trying to find new ways to stay up-to-date in their storytelling methods. One of the future projects Mater looks forward to is producing short videos, which is still in the planning phase. Medyascope is also setting up a podcast room to keep its technological infrastructure up-to-date. Moreover, Ünsal Ünlü also strengthens his infrastructure to broadcast simultaneously on different social media platforms. At the same time, he enriches the visual content of his live sessions with supplementary design applications. All these efforts are not only to keep abreast of the latest media technologies but also to attract the attention of the transmedia traversals by constructing an immersive news experience. Each discovery of a communication channel offers potential for new audiences, communities, forms of representation, hypertexts, and ways of interaction. Transmediality, in this sense, works as a guiding method and motivational reminder for independent journalists to find new media spaces to expand towards.

When asked whether they knew what transmediality is, Mater, Çakır, and Ünlü did not have a clue. Therefore, it is surprising to see that somehow these independent journalism initiatives organically formed collaborative, multimodal, and interactive news environments that embody transmedia narratives. However, although it may be surprising, it is most certainly not incomprehensible, especially in the context of journalism in Turkey. How can you practise journalism when your government denies your existence, takes away the mass medium out of your hand and restrains you with unethical regulations? Where these initiatives set up a home is away from the oppressive climate of the mainstream, in the (as yet) more free space of the Internet and social media network.

In their stories, we witness how their journeys start from scratch with few followers and grow into viable news sources that thousands of people follow daily. This growth did not happen overnight. Along the way, they aimed at delivering news to the masses and reaching their audiences on a deeper level. For that, these initiatives discovered efficient ways of using multiple media channels to their advantage by leaving footprints wherever the audience gathered. In other words, they constructed transmedia narratives to provide immersive news experiences to the public.

However, as seen in the way it has formed organically, this notion of transmediality cannot be observed only as a storytelling approach to news making but also as a way of life and method for these journalism initiatives to survive independently. In the complex habitat of journalism in Turkey, Bianet, Medyascope, and Ünsal Ünlü are only a few of the many who are trying to shape journalism culture into its new form. Within this new environment, the role of the medium, the profession, the audience, and the journalist are transforming. As explained in this chapter, transmediality, with both of its structural and value-laden aspects, plays a part in each stage of this changing culture.

## Notes

1 The interview with Nadire Mater was held on September 16, 2019, at the headquarters of Bianet in Beyoğlu, Istanbul.
2 Nadire Mater is a journalist, who worked as a reporter for local, national, and international magazines, newspapers, and radios. She is the chairwoman of IPS Communication Foundation and one of the co-founders of Bianet. It is possible to say that she dedicated most of her career to freedom of expression.
3 Ertuğrul Kürkçü is an author, a politician and a social activist, who co-founded the IPS Communication Foundation and Bianet. After his entry to the Turkish parliament, Kürkçü resigned from Bianet's project coordinator duties.
4 In 1993, Nadire Mater and Ertuğrul Kürkçü, along with feminist academician Dr. Şahika Yüksel, journalists Füsun Özbilgen and Tuğrul Eryılmaz, established The IPS Communication Foundation to "realise and support projects in the area of communication and development" (Bianet, 2007).
5 Although the foundation of the Internet was laid in the 1960s, the following developmental projects shaped it into the Internet as we know it today. Its infusion to our everyday practices was only available after mid-1990s, after Tim Berners-Lee's design of "the World Wide Web protocols that link hypertext documents into a working system" (Couldry, 2012, p. 2).
6 Erol Önderoğlu is a journalist, press freedom activist, and Turkey's representative of Reporters Without Borders (RSF). He is also a reporter of the quarterly media monitoring reports of Bianet.
7 In March 2015, a new article was added to the amendment of the Internet Law of Turkey. In this addition, Article 8A provides

> an additional procedure for removal of content and/or blocking of access in order to protect the right to life or security of life and property, national security and public order, public health and for the prevention of commission of crimes (Art. 8A(1)).
> (European Commission for Democracy Through Law (Venice Commission), 2016, p. 15)

8 Sevda Alankuş is an academician of communication, whose areas of interest are representation of women and minorities in the media, local and alternative media, and peace journalism. She is also an adviser of vocational news training in rights-based journalism in Atölye BIA. She regularly contributes to the publications of Bianet.
9 Ruşen Çakır is a journalist, who worked in several news media organisations such as Cumhuriyet, Milliyet, NTV, and Habertürk, to name a few.

He was let go of his author position in *Habertürk Newspaper* on 2016. He is the founder and currently the editorial director of *Medyascope.tv*. He also authored numerous books on Islamic religious networks in Turkey.

10 *Habertürk* is a Turkish newspaper that is currently owned by Ciner Group, which is one of the most powerful industrial conglomerates in Turkey.

11 The interview with Ruşen Çakır was held on September 6, 2019, at the main office of Medyascope in Şişli, Istanbul.

12 In the beginning, Medyascope's broadcasts were only limited to weekdays. However, starting from November 2019, the initiative also broadcasts on Saturdays with a plan to include Sundays in the near future.

13 In this cultural program, Burak Tatari talks with his guests about the favourite books they have read, series and movies they have watched and enjoyed, and the most interesting experiences they have had in the last two weeks and one day (Tatari, 2019).

14 Medyapod emerged in August 2018 as a joint initiative of a journalist, Tunca Öğreten, and an academician, Sarphan Uzunoğlu. Considering the rarity of podcast productions in Turkey, Medyapod engages with programmers who produce diverse content relating to technology, politics, culture, sports, and business. The main objective of this network is to promote the podcast listening habits in Turkey and become the pioneer of this form of media in Turkey (Medyapod, 2019; Medyascope, 2018).

15 ATV Europe TV channel hosts programs of news, business, culture, and many more to Turkish people living in European countries (ATV Avrupa, 2009).

16 In collaboration with the Helsinki Citizens' Assembly Turkey branch, Medyascope hosts Yurttaş Postası (Citizen Mail). The program covers various aspects of citizenship, such as freedom, rights, and democratisation.

17 In collaboration with the Social Rights Association, Medyascope hosts Sosyal Hukuk (Social Law). The program covers various aspects of social rights that enable a person to live a humanely dignified and safe life.

18 Medyascope also hosts programs that focus solely on children. One of these programs is Gündem Çocuk (The Agenda is Children). This program supports a holistic change for every child to lead a good and happy life in peace as a rightful, equal, free, and honourable individual. It is a continuing effort of Gündem Çocuk Association after its closure with a decree law in 2016.

19 Podiolab contributes to the development of podcast broadcasting in Turkish. It generates source of Turkish content, prepares audience surveys, and brings together broadcasters and listeners by following developments on podcast ecosystem (Podiolab, 2019).

20 He started his broadcasting career in 1982 at Çocuk Saati (The Children's Hour) radio program of TRT (The Turkish Radio and Television Corporation) and continued his career as a journalist since 1990. He worked as an announcer, reporter, editor, Ankara Representative, and Parliament reporter in TRT, CTV, NTV, and Haberturk television channels.

21 The interview with Ünsal Ünlü was held on August 23, 2019, at a place called Coffee Shop in Çankaya, Ankara.

22 On June 20, 2019, Ünlü was the guest of the weekly meetings held at the Press House of the Journalists Association in Ankara. The meetings were held within the scope of the Media for Democracy/Democracy for Media

program (M4D), funded by the European Union. In his talk about media transformation, Ünlü expressed how media was reconstructed along with Turkey's changing political power (Yavuz, 2019).

23 On October 25, 2019, Ünlü was the guest of the 42 Minutes seminar series conducted by the Psychology Department of Başkent University. His talk was titled "Haber, Psikolojiyi Bozar mı?" (Does the News Make One Depressed?) (Baskent U. Psikoloji, 2019).

24 On December 9, 2018, an independent event, titled TEDxMETUAnkara, was organised by the students of the Middle East Technical University. Ünlü took the stage in this event to question the conscience-mind relationship in the new age (TEDx Talks, 2019).

25 On May 20, 2019, Ünlü was the guest of an event in Izmir, titled Dönüm Noktası (Turning Point), which organises network meetings for entrepreneurs (Dönüm Noktası Izmir, 2015).

26 Media for Democracy is a project created by the Association of Journalists in January 2019. The project aims "to strengthen pluralist media and free press as a safeguard for democracy". Planned to continue until March 2022, the Association of Journalists takes on the responsibility to distribute the funds coming in from the European Union (EU) (Media for Democracy, 2019).

## References

ATV Avrupa. (2009, January 21). Homepage. Retrieved October 27, 2019, from ATV Avrupa website: http://www.atvavrupa.tv/

Baskent U. Psikoloji. (2019, October 25). Başkent Psikoloji ile 42' seminer dizisinin 25 Ekim 2019 Cuma günkü konuğu gazeteci Ünsal Ünlü @unsalunlu, "Haber, Psikolojiyi Bozar mı?" başlıklı bir konuşma yaptı. Retrieved October 30, 2019, from Twitter website: https://twitter.com/pskbaskent/status/1187713308016689152

Bianet. (2007, February 6). IPS communication foundation. Retrieved October 17, 2019, from Bianet website: http://bianet.org/english/sayfa/ips-communication-foundation

Bianet. (2011, November 25). About us. Retrieved October 17, 2019, from Bianet website:http://bianet.org/english/sayfa/independent-communication-network

Bianet. (2018a, January). bianet (@bianetorg). Retrieved October 20, 2019, from Instagram website: https://www.instagram.com/bianetorg/

Bianet. (2018b, May 8). Anasayfa. Retrieved October 18, 2019, from Toplumsal Cinsiyet Odaklı Habercilik Kütüphanesi website: http://www.haberd etoplumsalcinsiyet.org

Bianet. (2019). Proje Hakkında. Retrieved October 18, 2019, from Medya Gözlem Veritabanı v.1.5 website: https://medyagozlemveritabani.org/proje-hakkinda/

Çakır, R. (2015, August 20). Medyascope Hakkında. Retrieved October 19, 2019, from Medyascope website: https://medyascope.tv/hakkinda/

Canavilhas, J. (2013). Jornalismo Transmídia: Um Desafio ao Velho Ecossistema Midiático. In D. Renó, C. Campalans, S. Ruiz & V. Gosciola (Eds.),

*Periodismo Transmedia: Miradas múltiples* (pp. 53–68). Editorial Universidad del Rosario.

Couldry, N. (2012). *Media, Society, World: Social Theory and Digital Media
Practice.* Polity Press.

Diakopoulos, N. (2019). *Automating the News: How Algorithms Are Rewriting
the Media.* Harvard University Press.

Dönüm Noktası Izmir. (2015, January 8). Dönüm Noktası İzmir Vol53.
Retrieved November 1, 2019, from Facebook website: https://www.face
book.com/events/437409847032463/

Eldridge, S., II, & Franklin, B. (Eds.). (2018). *The Routledge Handbook of
Developments in Digital Journalism Studies.* Routledge.

England, A. (2019, September 17). Middle East tech shines in tough
neighbourhood. *Financial Times.* Retrieved from https://www.ft.com/
content/13d473f0-b50e-11e9-b2c2-1e116952691a

European Commission for Democracy through Law (Venice Commission).
(2016, June 15). *Turkey - Opinion on Law No. 5651 on regulation of publications on the internet and combating crimes committed by means of such
publication ('The Internet Law').* Retrieved from https://www.venice.coe.
int/webforms/documents/default.aspx?pdffile=CDL-AD(2016)011-e

Freeman, M. (2018a). New paths in transmediality as vast narratives. In
P. Brembilla & I. A. De Pascalis (Eds.), *Reading Contemporary Serial Television Universes: A Narrative Ecosystem Framework* (pp. 9–26). Routledge.

Freeman, M. (2018b). Transmedia charity: Constructing the ethos of the BBC's
Red Nose Day across media. In M. Freeman & R. R. Gambarato (Eds.),
*The Routledge Companion to Transmedia Studies* (pp. 306–313). Routledge.

Frischlich, L., Boberg, S., & Quandt, T. (2019). Comment sections as targets
of dark participation? Journalists' evaluation and moderation of deviant
user comments. *Journalism Studies, 20*(14), 2014–2033.

İbrişim, A. (2019, June 10). Türkiye'de podcast sektörünün geleceği. Retrieved
October 26, 2019, from Digital Age website: https://digitalage.com.tr/
turkiyede-podcast-sektorunun-gelecegi/

Jenkins, H. (2010). Transmedia education: The 7 principles revisited. *Confessions of an Aca-Fan, 21.* Retrieved from http://henryjenkins.org/2010/06/
transmedia_education_the_7_pri.html

Lemke, J. (2009). Multimodal genres and transmedia traversals: Social semiotics and the political economy of the sign. *Semiotica, 2009*(173), 173.

Lemke, J. (2010). Transmedia traversals: Marketing meaning and identity.
*Interdisciplinary Perspectives on Multimodality: Theory and Practice.*
Proceedings of the Third International Conference on Multimodality.
Campobasso: Palladino.

Media for Democracy. (2019, April 22). Who are we? Retrieved November 1,
2019, from Media for Democracy website: http://media4democracy.org/en/
page/who-are-we

Medyapod. (2019). Homepage. Retrieved October 22, 2019, from Medyapod
website: https://medyapod.com/

Medyascope. (2015). Künye. Retrieved October 24, 2019, from Medyascope website: https://medyascope.tv/kunye/

Medyascope. (2017, February). Medyascope is creating video-based journalism, live broadcasting, podcasts. Retrieved October 24, 2019, from Patreon website: https://www.patreon.com/medyascopetv

Medyascope. (2018). Medyapod. Retrieved October 22, 2019, from Medyascope website: https://medyascope.tv/author/medyapod/

Moloney, K. (2011). *Porting transmedia storytelling to journalism* (Master of Arts, University of Denver; A. Russell, Ed.). Retrieved from http://bit.ly/2DDTa03

Orman, S. (2019, April 9). Gazeteciler için Yeni Medya Atölyesi'ne Çağrı. Retrieved October 18, 2019, from Bianet website: https://bianet.org/bianet/print/207267-gazeteciler-icin-yeni-medya-atolyesi-ne-cagri

Podiolab. (2019). Ekibimiz. Retrieved October 26, 2019, from Podiolab website: http://podiolab.com/ekibimiz/

Tatari, B. (2019). 2hafta 1gün. Retrieved October 22, 2019, from Medyascope website: https://medyascope.tv/author/2hafta1gun/

TEDx Talks. (2019, February 19). Vicdan Rahatlatmanın Kısa Tarihi | Ünsal Ünlü | TEDxMETUAnkara. Retrieved November 1, 2019, from https://www.youtube.com/watch?v=TSuLHr_eXA4

Ünlü, Ü. (2019, Streamed live on Oct 25). Ekim 2019, Serbest Uçuş - Dertleşme. Retrieved October 30, 2019, from https://www.youtube.com/watch?v=xqWfrJzb4iU

Ünlü, Ü. (2009, August). ÜNSAL ÜNLÜ (@unsalunlu). Retrieved October 30, 2019, from Twitter website: https://twitter.com/unsalunlu

Ünlü, Ü. (2016, October). Ünsal Ünlü is creating Daily Podcasts and videos on the net. Retrieved November 1, 2019, from Patreon website: https://www.patreon.com/unsalunlu

Who owns the media in Turkey. (2016). Retrieved August 11, 2019, from Media Ownership Monitor website: https://turkey.mom-rsf.org/

Yavuz, S. (2019, June 20). Ünsal Ünlü ile "Medyanın Dönüşümü" konulu söyleşi gerçekleşti. Retrieved October 30, 2019, from Media for Democracy website: http://media4democracy.org/etkinlik/nsal-nl-ile-medyanin-dnsm-konulu-sylesi-gereklesti

Yılmaz, Z. (2018). *Yeni Türkiye'nin ruhu: hınç, tahakküm, muhtaçlaştırma.* İletişim Yayınları.

Ziegele, M. (2019). Reader commenting. In *The International Encyclopedia of Journalism Studies.* Wiley.

# 5   Conclusion

Attempts of understanding transmediality have revealed a variety of perspectives on a wide scale of disciplines both in the fictional and non-fictional realm. In order to define this term in the most effective sense, we need to observe, document, and analyse it in its many forms. This study is an attempt to map one of its perspectives. In a time where the idea of news making, reporting, and consuming gradually transform, this book positions transmediality as a way of discovery and survival for journalists, and a means of expression for the public. Its conclusion demonstrates how audiences and journalists, driven by common values and beliefs, can come together within alternative communication spaces in which they migrate from one medium to another. In the course of these transmedia experiences, a new culture of journalism comes to life. One that prioritises interactivity, collaboration, solidarity, and sincerity.

The investigation also reveals that the function of transmediality in Turkish journalism is gradually shifting from being only a commercial entity to becoming a political system for social change. In other words, transmediality is not utilised to maximise profits or loyalty but to construct a news environment where journalists can finance and practise their profession independent from the political pressures of the ruling government. Hence, it functions as a survival method for independent journalists to reach out to diverse audiences, get their messages across, and gain back the public trust. It can be observed as a framework of support that lies underneath these alternative attempts. When considered within this perspective, transmediality serves as a strategy of alternative mass communication in the absence of a functioning mainstream structure; constructs new paths of conflict resolution among a polarised society, forming new democratic communities that are built out of mutual respect; allows the journalist to influence his/her audience from a deeper and more emotional level; places the real-life events and the public in front and at the centre of news; and disempowers the government or any other force that may influence the process of news making.

Turkey, with its young population and dynamic future ahead, has countless means at its disposal to restore what is broken by the power wars of oppressive leaders. In this investigation, we observe three distinct journalism initiatives that put these means to use with the belief that good will arise from evil. In fact, the existence of these initiatives indicates that as journalists feel more trapped in this political pressure, they embrace their professional purpose even further. In light of this context, the search for the alternative is inevitable but, perhaps, this stance is not only limited to this specific geography.

Journalists all around the world, in some way or another, face political barriers while trying to do their jobs. In fact, the profession has faced such threats throughout its history. Perhaps, the never-ending global battle between journalists' autonomy and its oppressors is what gives the viewpoint offered in this research a universal angle. This study covers a perspective of transmediality that could also be applied to independent journalism initiatives of other contexts. It is possible to observe these independent attempts in a wide range of developing countries, and even in highly established democracies, where press freedom is limited, representation of the mainstream is insufficient; and click-bait journalism, fake news, alternative truths, and many more emerging obstacles get in the way of quality journalism. If we were to go even further, we may also foresee transmediality as the *sine qua non*[1] of all future independent journalism initiatives, therefore, their producers as transmedia journalists. One of the reasons for that is, as also demonstrated in this research, the traits of transmediality offer a news experience that the audiences of the 21st century demand. Another reason is that collaborative and decentralised news making experience through transmediality offers journalists the means of solidarity. The importance of solidarity in journalism cannot be explained better than a sentence from Lech Walesa's Nobel lecture,[2] which is the following: "He who once became aware of the power of solidarity and who breathed the air of freedom will not be crushed" (Walesa, 1985).

When we ask ourselves what more there is to discover through the lens of transmediality, we realise that the question drags us to an answer that is unpredictable. The scholarly works of transmedia studies so far work towards understanding its theory and practice within a variety of situations. However, the ongoing dynamic research shows that there are still undiscovered perspectives and untouched contexts within transmedia studies. This book, as the first of its kind, introduces

Turkey as a new context within the global debates of transmediality in journalism. Sharing previously unexamined cases from Turkey, it expands the knowledge of transmediality by diversifying its contextual borders.

In addition to its journalism context, Turkey also provides a valuable resource for transmedia studies in other practices, such as advertising, education, and charity. However, it is still an inchoate field that is rarely studied within the scholarly works of Turkish literature. Therefore, this book also serves as an invitation to fellow young scholars of Turkey, who wish to be a part of this constantly developing field of study and strengthen Turkey's position within its international discussions.

## Notes

1 *Sine qua non*, in this text, embodies the meaning of a thing that is absolutely necessary.
2 Lech Walesa is a leader of solidarity who, during the Cold War, fought for the dissemination of Soviet communism. In 1983, he received the Nobel Peace Prize and wrote his Nobel lecture speech to be read to the audience by his wife.

## Reference

Walesa, L. (1985). Nobel lecture. Retrieved 2019, from NobelPrize.org website: https://www.nobelprize.org/prizes/peace/1983/walesa/lecture/

# Index

Note: Page numbers followed by "n" denote endnotes.